THE CARTOON GUIDE TO

U.S. HISTORY

Volume I
1585·1865

Also available by Larry Gonick

The Cartoon Guide to Genetics
(with Mark Wheelis)

The Cartoon Guide to Computer Science

THE CARTOON GUIDE TO
U.S. HISTORY
Volume I
1585·1865

Larry Gonick

BARNES & NOBLE BOOKS
A DIVISION OF HARPER & ROW, PUBLISHERS
New York, Cambridge, Philadelphia
San Francisco, Washington, London, Mexico City
São Paulo, Singapore, Sydney

Portions of this work have appeared in *Whole Earth Review.*

FIRST EDITION

Library of Congress Cataloging-in-Publication Data

Gonick, Larry.
   The cartoon guide to U.S. History.

   (College outline series; CO/420)
   "Portions...have appeared in Whole earth review"—T.p.verso.
   Bibliography: p.
   Includes index.
   Contents: v. 1. 1585–1865.
   1. United States—History, Comic, satirical, etc.
I. Title   II. Title: Cartoon guide to United States history.   III. Series.
E178.4.G66   1987   973'.0207   85-45200
ISBN 0-06-460420-9 (pbk. : v. 1)

87 88 89 90 91 MPC 10 9 8 7 6 5 4 3 2 1

CONTENTS

·PROLOGUE·

WHO FOUND IT?

MERICA WAS DISCOVERED SO LONG AGO THAT NO ONE CAN REMEMBER THE DETAILS...

IT APPEARS TO HAVE HAPPENED ABOUT 15,000 YEARS AGO, WHEN A TRIBE OF SIBERIANS OR MONGOLIANS CROSSED A LAND BRIDGE THAT JOINED ASIA TO ALASKA AT THE TIME.

THE LAND BRIDGE SANK, AND THE VISITORS STAYED...

SOME 2000 YEARS AGO, A
CHINESE SHIP DROPPED ANCHOR
OFF SOUTHERN CALIFORNIA —
LITERALLY "DROPPED": THE
ANCHOR IS STILL THERE...

ON A.D 985 THE
VIKING *ERIC THE
RED* LANDED ON
A GLACIAL BLOCK
HE PROMOTED AS
"GREENLAND."
HIS SON *LEIF
ERICSSON* SAILED TO
THE AMERICAN MAIN-
LAND, NAMING IT
"VINLAND." THE
VINLAND COLONY
FAILED, DUE TO
A SHORTAGE
OF "VIN."

THERE'S ALSO A CONFUSED, POETIC ACCOUNT OF A
POSSIBLE ATLANTIC CROSSING BY AN IRISH MONK...

2

CHRISTOPHER COLUMBUS WAS
THE MAN IN THE RIGHT
PLACE AT THE RIGHT TIME.
HIS "DISCOVERY" CAME IN 1492,
JUST AS EUROPE WAS EMERGING
FROM THE MIDDLE AGES.

FOR HUNDREDS OF YEARS, EUROPEAN
CHRISTIANS HAD BEEN CRUSADING
AGAINST MUSLIMS... IN THAT VERY
SAME 1492, THE LAST MUSLIMS WERE
EXPELLED FROM SPAIN... BUT
CENTURIES OF CONTACT HAD LEFT
THE SPANIARDS WITH TWO THINGS:
A TASTE FOR SPICY ARAB FOOD,
AND THE KNOWLEDGE THAT SPICES
WERE THE MOST PROFITABLE ITEM
OF COMMERCE KNOWN TO MAN !!

THE NATION
THAT CONTROLS
PEPPER WILL CONTROL
THE WORLD!

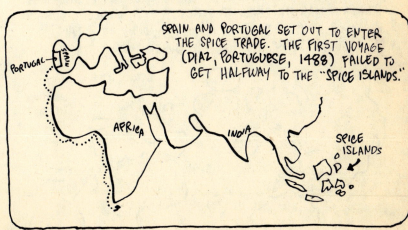

SPAIN AND PORTUGAL SET OUT TO ENTER
THE SPICE TRADE. THE FIRST VOYAGE
(DIAZ, PORTUGUESE, 1488) FAILED TO
GET HALFWAY TO THE "SPICE ISLANDS."

PORTUGAL — SPAIN

AFRICA

INDIA

SPICE
ISLANDS

SPAIN, HOPING FOR A SHORT-
CUT, SPONSORED COLUMBUS,
WHOSE IDEA WAS TO REACH
THE EAST BY HEADING WEST.

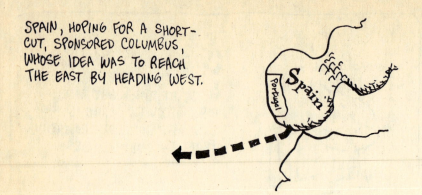

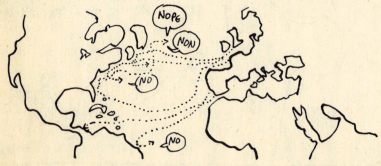

WHEN THE TRUTH WAS REALIZED — THAT AN UNKNOWN, SPICELESS
CONTINENT WAS BLOCKING THE ROUTE — A WHOLE INDUSTRY
SPRANG UP TRYING TO FIND A WAY AROUND IT. THIS
WAS CALLED "SEARCHING FOR THE NORTHWEST PASSAGE."

THE SPANIARDS HAD ANOTHER IDEA...
THE IDEA OF COLONIZATION... THEY
CONQUERED MOST OF CENTRAL AND
SOUTH AMERICA, LOOTED THE GOLD
OF MEXICO AND PERU, ESTABLISHED
SLAVE PLANTATIONS IN THE
CARIBBEAN, AND MADE SPAIN THE
MOST SPLENDID NATION IN EUROPE.

SPAIN'S RIVALS, ENGLAND, FRANCE, AND HOLLAND, ALL WATCHED
JEALOUSLY.

IT'S JOLLY
UNFAIR!

BUT THEY WERE STILL TOO POOR, POWERLESS, OR PREOCCUPIED
TO MAKE A MOVE. IT WAS ALMOST 100 YEARS AFTER
COLUMBUS BEFORE ENGLAND PLANTED HER FIRST COLONY
IN THE NEW WORLD...

5

...AND THAT IS WHERE OUR STORY BEGINS...

The arriual of the Englifhemen
in Virginia.

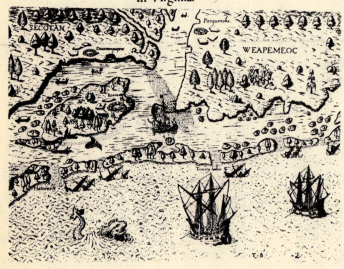

· CHAPTER ONE ·

IN WHICH ENGLAND PLANTS THIS AND THAT

IN 1585, THE FIRST ENGLISH COLONISTS ARRIVED ON ROANOKE ISLAND, VIRGINIA.

(NOW IT'S NORTH CAROLINA; THEN IT WAS VIRGINIA.)

THE COLONY WAS SUPPOSED TO BE A PROFIT-MAKING ENTERPRISE, BUT IT WAS FAR FROM OBVIOUS WHAT VIRGINIA'S SOURCE OF WEALTH WAS SUPPOSED TO BE...

ONE THING VIRGINIA DEFINITELY HAD WAS A POPULATION. IT WENT BACK AT LEAST AS FAR AS THE LAST ICE AGE, AND, AT THIS POINT, SAW NO REASON TO MAKE WAY FOR A SECOND SET OF FIRST FAMILIES...

BY 1590, THE ROANOKE COLONY HAD BECOME THE LOST COLONY.

NOTHING ELSE HAPPENED UNTIL 1602, WHEN A SEA CAPTAIN
WITH THE MUSICAL NAME OF BARTHOLOMEW GOSNOLD
ARRIVED, JUST AFTER DROPPING THE NAME "CAPE COD"
ON NEW ENGLAND'S BIGGEST SPIT.

PREFERRING THE FRAGRANCE OF WILDFLOWERS TO THE AROMA
OF DRYING CODFISH, GOSNOLD DECIDED TO ORGANIZE A
SECOND EFFORT IN VIRGINIA. IN 1607, 100 COLONISTS
ARRIVED, BUILT A FORT, AND CALLED IT JAMESTOWN.

DESPITE THE FORT, 2/3 OF THE
SETTLERS DIED, MOSTLY OF
DISEASE AND STARVATION,
INCLUDING CAPT. GOSNOLD.
THE REST LIVED ON HANDOUTS
FROM THE "ENEMY."

9

AFTER THIS SECOND DISASTER, THE COLONY'S SPONSORS HAD AN ATTACK OF CONFUSION. WHAT WAS VIRGINIA GOOD FOR, ANYWAY??

LET'S LOOK ON THE BRIGHT SIDE!!

RE-EVALUATING THEIR GOALS, THEY CONSOLED THEMSELVES WITH THE THOUGHT THAT VIRGINIA WAS HELPING DISPOSE OF ENGLAND'S "SURPLUS POPULATION."

THEY QUICKLY PACKED OFF 500 MORE VOLUNTEERS, OF WHOM MORE THAN 400 PROMPTLY DIED.

INSTANT SUCCESS!

WHAT ARE THEY TRYING TO GROW HERE?

CROSSES?

Not everyone was willing to lie down and be disposed of, so Capt. **JOHN SMITH** led a war party to seize the Indians' stores. Captured by the Powhatans, his head was on the block, when the princess **POCAHONTAS** intervened. Smith thought it must be love, but who knows? He didn't speak Powhatan...

STILL, HOW CAN YOU TRUST A MAN WHO CALLS HIMSELF "JOHN SMITH"?

SMITH WAS SPARED... POCAHONTAS MARRIED THE ENGLISHMAN JOHN ROLFE... AND THE POWHATANS MADE A TREATY OF FRIENDSHIP WITH THE VIRGINIANS.

SO THE COLONY WOULD SURVIVE... BUT WOULD IT THRIVE? WHAT COULD THEY PLANT ON THIS PLANTATION (BESIDES CORPSES, THAT IS)? THEY TRIED COFFEE, SUGAR CANE, BANANAS... UNTIL FINALLY JOHN ROLFE HIT ON **TOBACCO**, A NATIVE WEED.

THE RESPONSE IN ENGLAND WAS SENSATIONAL, BEYOND ANYONE'S IMAGINATION— IN FACT, YOU COULD BARELY SEE IT.

KAF!

HWAK!

THE DEMAND FOR TOBACCO WAS SO GREAT THAT VIRGINIANS BEGAN TO HAVE HOPE. TOBACCO PLANTATIONS SPROUTED EVERYWHERE, AS THE INDIANS' SACRED WEED BECAME THE COLONY'S STAPLE CROP.

NOW THEY'VE BECOME INSANELY RELIGIOUS!

THE STUFF WAS EVERYWHERE... IT DOMINATED VIRGINIA'S ECONOMY FOR CENTURIES. THROUGHOUT THE COLONIAL PERIOD, TOBACCO WAS USED AS MONEY IN VIRGINIA!

CAN YOU CHANGE A HOGSHEAD?

EVENTUALLY, ALL AMERICA BECAME ADDICTED TO SMOKING, SNIFFING, OR CHEWING. AS LATE AS 1832, AN ENGLISH VISITOR OBSERVED THAT CHEWING AND SPITTING WERE UNIVERSAL IN AMERICA.

IT'S A PTOO PATRIOTIC DUTY!

(EVEN TODAY THE TOBACCO INDUSTRY RECEIVES GOVERNMENT SUBSIDIES!)

IF ONLY THE DEAD COULD WORK!

THE DEMAND FOR TOBACCO ALSO CREATED A DEMAND FOR LABOR. THE INDIANS WEREN'T WILLING TO SERVE THE PEOPLE WHO WERE PLOWING UP THE HUNTING GROUNDS, AND THERE WEREN'T ENOUGH ENGLISH TO GO AROUND.

AND SO, IN 1619, THE FIRST BLACK SLAVES WERE PURCHASED.

SLAVE LABOR HAD ITS ADVANTAGES: THE SLAVE, BEING BOUND FOR LIFE, WOULD NEVER QUIT TO START HIS OR HER OWN PLANTATION... SLAVES COULD BE IMPORTED AT WILL, WHEREAS WHITES ONLY CAME TO VIRGINIA WHEN THEY WANTED TO*... SO SLAVEOWNING SPREAD.

IT'S AS ADDICTIVE AS TOBACCO!

* MORE OR LESS... SEE BELOW.

14

IRONICALLY, AMERICA'S DEMOCRATIC INSTITUTIONS BEGAN IN THE SAME YEAR AS SLAVERY. IN 1619, VIRGINIA TAXPAYERS ORGANIZED THE **HOUSE OF BURGESSES,** COLONIAL AMERICA'S FIRST ELECTED LEGISLATURE.

WHAT IS A "BURGESS"?

I DON'T KNOW WHAT IT IS, BUT I KNOW WHAT IT ISN'T...

THE ONLY ELIGIBLE VOTERS WERE WHITE, MALE LANDOWNERS.

EVEN THAT WAS TOO DEMOCRATIC FOR KING JAMES. HE DECIDED TO ABOLISH THE HOUSE OF BURGESSES, BUT DIED BEFORE MAKING THE MOVE. THE BUDDING DEMOCRACY SURVIVED, AND VIRGINIA'S BASIC WAY OF LIFE WAS ESTABLISHED.

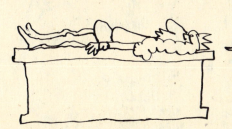

A SLAVING, CARCINOGENIC COLONY WITH REPRESENTATIVE GOVERNMENT!

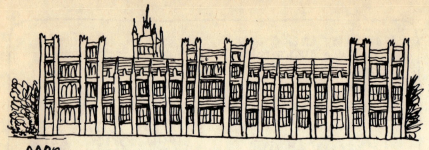

Why, YOU MAY ASK, WOULD ANY SANE PERSON LEAVE ENGLAND FOR VIRGINIA? GOOD QUESTION!! WELL, IT SEEMS THAT "MERRIE ENGLAND" WAS LOSING ITS SENSE OF HUMOR, AS LANDLORDS EVICTED FARMERS BY THE THOUSANDS, FORCING THEM TO FACE SOME VERY TOUGH CHOICES...

THERE AREN'T ANY JOBS IN THE CITY...

IF YOU GO TOO FAR INTO DEBT, IT'S JAIL FOR SURE!

I'M TOO PROUD TO BEG...

SO I STOLE A LOAF OF BREAD AND WAS SENTENCED TO DEATH...

THEN THEY OFFERED ME A CHOICE BETWEEN HANGING AND VIRGINIA...

I CHOSE HANGING.

I'D RATHER BE IN HELL IN TWO MINUTES THAN VIRGINIA IN 30 DAYS!

TRULY, WE ARE BLEST WITH A BENEVOLENT GOVERNMENT!

ON TOP OF THIS, THE CHURCH OF ENGLAND WAS **ESTABLISHED**—MEANING TAX-SUPPORTED AND GOVERNMENT-REGULATED. ITS MINISTERS WERE LICENSED, AND THEIR SALARIES WERE PAID BY THE STATE.

ALL OTHER CHURCHES WERE BANNED BY LAW.

THAT MAKES SENSE! HOW CAN MORE THAN ONE RELIGION BE TRUE?

HOW ABOUT

LESS THAN

ONE?

EVEN SO, ALL MANNER OF UNLICENSED CHURCHES SPRANG UP: BAPTISTS, QUAKERS, PRESBYTERIANS, FIFTH MONARCHISTS, THE BROTHERHOOD OF LOVE... THESE WERE THE PROTEST MOVEMENTS OF THE EARLY 1600'S.

WE DON'T HAVE RADIO STATIONS OR NEWSPAPERS, ONLY PULPITS!

17

MARTYRDOM WITHIN LIMITS, THAT'S MY MOTTO!

AS THE GOVERNMENT CRACKED DOWN, MANY OF THE OUTLAWED SECTS FLED THE COUNTRY, OFTEN TO TOLERANT HOLLAND.

ONE OF THESE SECTS, NOW KNOWN AS THE **PILGRIMS**, SPENT TEN YEARS (1609-1619) IN HOLLAND. THEY FOUND THE TOLERANT ATMOSPHERE THERE INTOLERABLE... SO THE PILGRIMS HIRED A SHIP, THE **MAYFLOWER**, AND SAILED FOR AMERICA IN 1620.

IS THERE RELIGIOUS PERSECUTION IN AMERICA?

GIVE ME SIX MONTHS!

While still on shipboard, the colonists signed the

MAYFLOWER COMPACT,

a written agreement to abide by the rules of the colony.

The compact's historical significance is in what it implied:

⇊

That a government depends on the consent of the governed — a radical concept in 1620.

WHAT HAPPENED TO THE DIVINE RIGHT OF KINGS?

Landing in Massachusetts, the Pilgrims immediately found themselves triply blessed:

First, the area had just been depopulated by plague. There was no one to fight.

Second, only half the colonists died the first winter.

IN VIRGINIA, THAT'D BE A POPULATION EXPLOSION...

Third, the amazing Squanto: a local Patuxent, Squanto had been kidnapped to England in 1616, missed the plague, and returned in 1619. He spoke fluent English.

FORSOOTH, WHAT'S HAPPENIN'?

19

THANKS MAINLY TO
SQUANTO'S FARMING TIPS,
THE PILGRIMS REAPED
A BUMPER CROP IN 1622.
THEY CELEBRATED WITH
THE FIRST THANKSGIVING,
INVITING THE INDIANS TO
SHARE THE FEAST.

OR, FROM
OUR POINT
OF VIEW,
THE *LAST*
THANKSGIVING!

WHEW...

OOG!

AND FROM
OUR POINT OF VIEW?

DESPITE THE FRIENDLY ATMOSPHERE,
THE PILGRIMS TRIED TO KEEP THE
INDIANS IN AWE. FOR EXAMPLE,
THEY HINTED THAT THEY COULD
BRING BACK THE PLAGUE, IF
NECESSARY.

THE ENDE
JUSTIFIETH
THE MEANS...

BUT IT APPEARED THAT THE PILGRIMS JUST COULDN'T GET AWAY FROM IT ALL! IN 1626 A WILD MAN NAMED **THOMAS MORTON** SET UP SHOP NEARBY AT "MERRYMOUNT" (A NAME WITH DEFINITE GYNECOLOGICAL OVERTONES IN THOSE DAYS), AND HOISTED A MAYPOLE.

A PAGAN ABOMINATION!

PLYMOUTH'S PINT-SIZED CAPTAIN **MYLES STANDISH** MADE A SPECIAL TRIP TO TEAR IT DOWN...

* *

OTHER NEIGHBORS IN THOSE QUAINT DAYS INCLUDED VARIOUS FISHERMEN UP IN NEW HAMPSHIRE AND MAINE, SAMUEL MAVERICK, ANCESTOR OF TEXANS, AND WILLIAM BLAXTON OF SHAWMUT, WHO TRAINED A BULL TO RIDE, BECAUSE HE'D FORGOTTEN TO BRING A HORSE...

EE-HAW!

IN 1630 CAME THE DELUGE: 1000 PURITANS, WITH CATTLE, HORSES, SEED, TOOLS, AND BIBLES, LANDED NEAR MODERN BOSTON AND FOUNDED THE COLONY OF **MASSACHUSETTS BAY.**

THE PURITANS ARE COMING!

WHATEVER THEY ARE!

A **PURITAN** WAS SOMEONE TRYING TO "PURIFY" THE ESTABLISHED CHURCH FROM WITHIN (WHEREAS THE PILGRIMS WERE "SEPARATISTS," WHO HAD SPLIT AWAY COMPLETELY).

THE DIFFERENCE BETWEEN A PURITAN AND A SEPARATIST? ABOUT £2000 A YEAR!

THE PURITANS INCLUDED MANY RICH FAMILIES— WHILE SEPARATISTS GENERALLY HAD LESS TO LOSE.

WHATEVER THEIR DIFFERENCES, PURITANS AND PILGRIMS AGREED: IN THEIR COLONIES, THE LAWS WOULD BE BASED ON OLD TESTAMENT LAWS: NO WORK ON THE SABBATH, AN EAR FOR AN EAR, DEATH TO WITCHES, THAT SORT OF THING.

ABSOLUTELY NO JIVE!!

THE MASSACHUSETTS MEN SHARPENED THEIR EAR SNIPS, KICKED OUT THOMAS MORTON, FOUNDED HARVARD, SWALLOWED MAINE AND NEW HAMPSHIRE, AND DECLARED ALL NEW ENGLAND A **PURITAN COMMONWEALTH**. IT HAD A TAX-SUPPORTED CHURCH WITH LICENSED MINISTERS, AND NO OTHER CHURCHES WERE ALLOWED!!

IS THERE ANOTHER WAY?

23

SUDDENLY IT BECAME A TREND
TO ESCAPE RELIGIOUS
PERSECUTION BY FOUNDING
AN AMERICAN COLONY.

IT'S CHIC!

LORD BALTIMORE MADE MARYLAND A CATHOLIC HAVEN IN 1634.

ROGER WILLIAMS FLED FROM RELIGIOUS PERSECUTION IN BOSTON (!) TO FOUND RHODE ISLAND IN 1635. WILLIAMS BELIEVED IN COMPLETE SEPARATION OF CHURCH AND STATE, AND RHODE ISLAND BECAME A HAVEN OF RELIGIOUS FREEDOM.

JEWS? YOU'D LET IN JEWS?

JEWS AND TURKS!

IN FACT, OF THE BUNCH OF COLONIES FOUNDED IN THE 1630'S, ONLY CONNECTICUT, IN 1636, WASN'T FORMED WITH THE EXPRESS PURPOSE OF GETTING OUT FROM UNDER SOMEBODY'S THUMB.

⊸○ CHAPTER 2 ○⊸
NEW COLONIES AND BABY CHICKENS

As YOU MAY HAVE NOTICED, THE FIRST AMERICAN COLONIES WERE NOT EXACTLY CONCEIVED IN LIBERTY. TWO OF THEM WERE RIGIDLY PURITAN, WHILE THE OTHER WAS ESSENTIALLY A COMMERCIAL VENTURE, AT FIRST.

FREEDOM OF THE PRESS? THE CIDER PRESS, MAYBE!

SO WHERE DO WE FIRST HEAR ABOUT THE "LIBERTIES OF ENGLISHMEN"?

THE ANSWER SEEMS TO BE —

WHEN THE RELIGIOUS FRICTION BETWEEN PURITANS AND ESTABLISHMENT EXPLODED INTO THE **ENGLISH CIVIL WAR** (1642 - 1648).

FREEDOM OF THE PRESS, FREEDOM OF WORSHIP, A VOTE FOR "THE POOREST HE" — TOO BAD IT WASN'T THE OFFICIAL PURITAN PROGRAM.

THESE WERE THE DEMANDS OF A SMALL GROUP OF ANTI-ESTABLISHMENT AGITATORS, THE **LEVELLERS.**

"FREEBORN JOHN" LILBURNE, LEVELLER IDEA MAN ←

THE LEVELLERS SPREAD THE WORD... AND SOON THEIR SLOGANS WERE ON THE LIPS — AND PETITIONS — OF THE PURITAN ARMY'S RANK AND FILE, THE "ROUNDHEADS."

IT MADE PERFECT SENSE — WHAT ELSE SHOULD THEY FIGHT FOR?

BIGGER WIGS FOR THE COMMON HE?

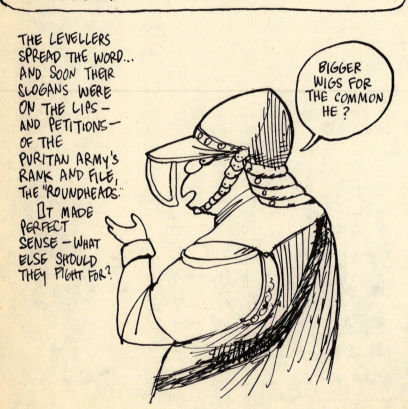

TOO MANY KOOKS SPOIL THE BROTH!

SECRET LEVELLER PRESSES CRANKED OUT PROPAGANDA... LEVELLER AGITATORS STIRRED UP THE ARMY...

IT WAS TOO MUCH FOR THE PURITAN LEADERS...

THEY SMASHED THE LEVELLER ORGANIZATION AND SENT THE TROOPS TO IRELAND.

'BYE!

BUT FRESH IDEAS ARE LIKE BABY CHICKENS: HARD TO PUT BACK IN THE SHELL, ONCE THEY'VE HATCHED.

ACTUALLY, FRESH IDEAS USUALLY LIVE A LOT LONGER THAN BABY CHICKENS...

27

BUT BACK TO THE CIVIL WAR: THE ROUNDHEADS DEFEATED THE CAVALIERS, AND IN 1649 THEY REMOVED KING CHARLES' HEAD.

HE WASN'T DETACHED ENOUGH!

IN 1654, SOME DISGUSTED DEMOCRATS LEFT VIRGINIA TO FOUND THEIR OWN COLONY— NORTH CAROLINA.

GIVE ME *LEVELLER* GROUND!

AS MASSACHUSETTS CHEERED, HORDES OF NOBLEMEN SCURRIED TO VIRGINIA FOR SAFETY. (IT'S STILL KNOWN AS "THE CAVALIER STATE.")

HM! I THOUGHT THAT MEANT MY DEVIL-MAY-CARE ATTITUDE!

THEN, IN 1660, ENGLAND'S PURITAN EXPERIMENT COLLAPSED. THE THRONE WAS RESTORED TO CHARLES II, WHILE PURITAN REFUGEES FLED TO BOSTON.

WATCH OUT! WIGS ARE MAKING A COMEBACK!

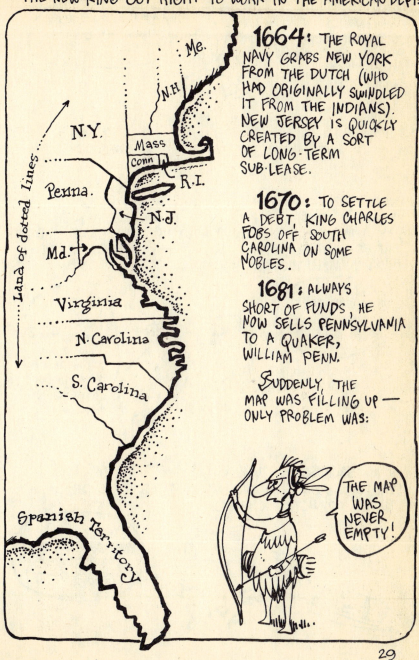

1664: THE ROYAL NAVY GRABS NEW YORK FROM THE DUTCH (WHO HAD ORIGINALLY SWINDLED IT FROM THE INDIANS). NEW JERSEY IS QUICKLY CREATED BY A SORT OF LONG-TERM SUB-LEASE.

1670: TO SETTLE A DEBT, KING CHARLES FOBS OFF SOUTH CAROLINA ON SOME NOBLES.

1681: ALWAYS SHORT OF FUNDS, HE NOW SELLS PENNSYLVANIA TO A QUAKER, WILLIAM PENN.

SUDDENLY, THE MAP WAS FILLING UP — ONLY PROBLEM WAS:

THE MAP WAS NEVER EMPTY!

Me.

N.H

N.Y.

Mass

Conn

R.I.

Penna.

N.J.

Md.

Virginia

N. Carolina

S. Carolina

Land of dotted lines

Spanish Territory

29

OF COURSE, EVERY NEWLY COLONIZED ACRE HAD TO BE TAKEN AWAY FROM SOMEBODY.

IF NOT BY FORCE, THEN BY GOOD, HONEST TRICKERY!

A COUPLE OF EXAMPLES:

PEACEABLE PENNSYLVANIA PURCHASED A STRETCH OF THE DELAWARE RIVER, AS FAR AS "A MAN CAN WALK IN A DAY AND A HALF." WHEN SURVEYING TIME CAME, THE WHITES BLAZED A TRAIL, SET UP REFRESHMENT STANDS, HIRED A MARATHONER, AND MADE IT 64 MILES!

NOW WHERE ARE **WE** SUPPOSED TO GO?

I DON'T KNOW, BUT IT'LL TAKE MORE THAN A DAY AND A HALF TO GET THERE...

IN MASSACHUSETTS, WHERE THEY WENT BY THE BOOK (THE LAW BOOK), AN INDIAN'S LAND COULD BE SEIZED IF HE WAS CONVICTED OF ANY CRIME.

PRACTICING YOUR OWN RELIGION IS A CRIME IN MASSACHUSETTS!

IN 1676 THE COLONIES EXPERIENCED SEVERE GROWING PAINS.

THEY GROW, WE HAVE THE PAIN!

"PHILIP'S WAR":

IN MASSACHUSETTS, THE NARRAGANSETT **METACOMET** ("KING PHILIP") LED A GUERRILLA WAR AGAINST THE WHITES. THIS RESULTED IN THE NEAR-EXTERMINATION OF THE NARRAGANSETTS.

METACOMET'S HEAD BECAME A MUSEUM PIECE AT PLYMOUTH.

BACON'S REVOLT:

IN VIRGINIA, A CIVIL WAR ERUPTED WHEN GOV. BERKELEY TRIED TO STOP FARMERS FROM "REMOVING" INDIANS. THE INFURIATED FARMERS BURNED JAMESTOWN.

THEY WANT SLAVES ON INDIAN LAND IN THE NAME OF DEMOCRACY! MIND·BOGGLING!

31

BACK IN ENGLAND, THE VIRGINIA UPROAR SOUNDED LIKE REVOLUTION — AND THIS WAS 1676, A HUNDRED YEARS AHEAD OF SCHEDULE!

AND VIRGINIA'S ONE OF MY BETTER PROPERTIES!

CHARLES II

MASSACHUSETTS, MEANWHILE, WAS CHRONICALLY DISOBEDIENT. THE BAY COLONY HARBORED THE KILLERS OF CHARLES I, BARRED THE KING'S CHURCH, AND IGNORED THE KING'S TAXES AND REGULATIONS. WHAT WAS A KING TO DO? COLONIES WERE SUPPOSED TO BE LOYAL AND PROFITABLE!!

THESE ROBES ARE EXPENSIVE!

THE KING DISSOLVED THE MASS. GOVERNMENT AND SENT OVER A ROYAL GOVERNOR, WHO WAS QUICKLY JAILED BY THE BOSTON MOB.

MAKE THAT THE "LEGENDARY BOSTON MOB"!

NEVERTHELESS, THE CROWN KEPT THE COLONY, OPENED AN ANGLICAN CHURCH, AND ENDED THE PURITAN MONOPOLY IN MASSACHUSETTS FOREVER.

THIS IS THE DEVIL'S WORK!

IN THIS CLIMATE OF MORAL DEGENERATION, THE PEOPLE BEGAN SEEING WITCHES AT WORK... THE SALEM WITCHCRAFT TRIALS SENT 20 HUMANS AND TWO DOGS TO THEIR DEATHS, BEFORE THINGS CALMED DOWN.

THERE. NOW I FEEL BETTER!

...WHICH BRINGS
US TO THE YEAR

1700

(AT LAST!
WHEW!)

MORE
THAN A CHANGE
OF CENTURY, IT
WAS A CHANGE
OF MIND... "THE
ENLIGHTENMENT."

RELIGIOUS WARS
DIED DOWN...
LOGIC PREVAILED...
"THE LIGHT OF THE
MIND REPLACED THE
FIRE IN THE BELLY."

HADN'T NEWTON'S LAW OF
GRAVITATION (1687) PROVED
THAT THE HEAVENS WERE
DRIVEN BY EQUATIONS?

EVERYWHERE, THE
UNTHINKABLE WAS
THOUGHT...

GOD
IS AN
EQUATION!

IN AMERICA, THE TREND
COULD BE SUMMED UP IN
TWO WORDS:

BENJAMIN FRANKLIN.

BORN IN BOSTON IN **1706**, FRANKLIN GREW UP WITH THE NEW CENTURY.

FOR STARTERS, HE HORRIFIED HIS PURITAN PARENTS BY BECOMING A **DEIST**, WHICH MEANT THAT HE BELIEVED IN A SORT OF ABSTRACT GOD, NOT A BEARDED JEHOVAH IN THE SKY.
ON HIS OWN WORDS:

"**S**INCE THERE IS IN ALL MEN SOMETHING LIKE A NATURAL PRINCIPLE WHICH ENCLINES THEM TO DEVOTION OR THE WORSHIP OF SOME UNSEEN POWER... THEREFORE, I THINK IT SEEMS REQUIRED OF ME, AND MY DUTY AS A MAN, TO PAY DIVINE REGARDS TO **SOMETHING.**"

AND: ⬇

"**A**S TO JESUS OF NAZARETH,... I HAVE SOME DOUBTS OF HIS DIVINITY, THO' IT IS A QUESTION I DO NOT DOGMATIZE UPON... I SEE NO HARM, HOWEVER, IN ITS BEING BELIEVED, IF THAT BELIEF HAS THE GOOD CONSEQUENCE, AS IT PROBABLY HAS, OF MAKING HIS DOCTRINES MORE RESPECTED AND BETTER OBSERVED."

"DOUBTS"? "NO HARM"? "IF"? "PROBABLY"? PERFORATE HIS TONGUE!

FRANKLIN BROKE INTO PRINT AS A TEENAGER, LAMPOONING MINISTERS IN THE PAGES OF THE **NEW ENGLAND COURANT**, AMERICA'S FIRST "UNDERGROUND" NEWSPAPER (1722).

EEK AND EVIL!

BANNED IN BOSTON, BENJAMIN MOVED TO THE FREER AIR OF PHILADELPHIA IN 1723.

THERE HE WENT INTO THE PRINTING BUSINESS. (PRINTSHOPS WERE POPPING UP EVERYWHERE, AS THE COLONIAL POPULATION WAS NOW BIG ENOUGH TO SUPPORT THEM.)

HOW FREE WAS THE PRESS? WELL, UNTIL **1733**, EVEN PRINTING THE TRUTH COULD LAND YOU IN JAIL, IF YOU INSULTED THE RIGHT PEOPLE.

ALMOST EVERYTHING ABOUT ME IS LIBELOUS!

THAT YEAR, NEW YORK PUBLISHER **PETER ZENGER** WAS ARRESTED FOR LIBELING THE COLONIAL GOVERNOR.

ZENGER'S LAWYER PERSUADED THE JURY TO SET ZENGER FREE, ON THE GROUNDS THAT TRUTH CAN'T BE LIBEL — AND A GREAT PRINCIPLE WAS BORN:

THE PRESS IS FREE, THE LAWYER ISN'T!

BUT BACK TO FRANKLIN ⟹

TO MAKE A LONG STORY SHORT, FRANKLIN GREW UP TO BECOME AMERICA'S MOST SUCCESSFUL PRINTER, RICH ENOUGH TO RETIRE FROM THE BUSINESS AT AGE 42.

IT'S THE AMERICAN WAY—OR AT LEAST, MY WAY!

HIS NEXT CAREER MOVE WAS TO BECOME AMERICA'S FIRST WORLD-CLASS SCIENTIST.

IN THE THEN-HOT FIELD OF ELECTRICITY, FRANKLIN PROVED THE FAMOUS FACT THAT LIGHTNING BOLTS ARE ELECTRIC SPARKS, AND (JUST FOR FUN) HE AND HIS FRIENDS USED TO ELECTROCUTE TURKEYS. (I DIDN'T MAKE ANY OF THIS UP!)

IN A MORE PRACTICAL VEIN, FRANKLIN INVENTED THE LIGHTNING ROD, THE STORAGE BATTERY, AN ENERGY-EFFICIENT STOVE, AND BIFOCALS.

HE COULD DO EVERYTHING EXCEPT RELAX !!

AND AS A PUBLIC CITIZEN, HE PROMOTED A VOLUNTEER FIRE DEPARTMENT, A NON-SECTARIAN COLLEGE (LATER TO BE THE U. OF PENN.), A PHILOSOPHICAL SOCIETY, A VOLUNTEER MILITIA, PAVED ROADS, STREET SWEEPING... AND HE STILL HAD TIME TO COIN CLEVER SAYINGS — ALL BEFORE **1755**.

A PENNY SAVED IS A PENNY EARNED!

TIME IS MONEY!

EARLY TO BED AND EARLY TO RISE...

: WHEW : JUST BE GLAD YOU DON'T WORK FOR HIM!

NOW YOU HAVE SOME IDEA HOW FAR THE COLONIES HAD COME BY MID-CENTURY.

A VOTE FOR THE "POOREST HE"? STILL FAR FROM IT!

SH!

NOT TO MENTION THE "RICHEST SHE"!

FREEDOM OF RELIGION? EVEN MASSACHUSETTS HAD LOOSENED UP, WHILE RHODE ISLAND AND PENNSYLVANIA WELCOMED ALMOST EVERY SECT. FRANKLIN DONATED MONEY TO THEM ALL.

NO WONDER THEY TOLERATE ME!

FREEDOM OF THE PRESS? THEN AS NOW, AS FREE AS THE NEAREST ATTORNEY!

AT LEAST THERE IS A PRESS!

AND WHERE THERE ARE LAWYERS, YOU'RE SURE TO FIND A GOVERNMENT OF LAWS... LAWSUITS... AND PROPERTY IN HEAPS... AND THAT BRINGS US TO THE NEXT CHAPTER...

ALSO, YOU CAN EAT THE MEAT!

THE CLOSEST THING THE AMERICAN INDIANS HAD TO MONEY WAS **WAMPUM:** BLUE AND WHITE BEADS PAINSTAKINGLY CARVED FROM CLAMSHELLS. UNLIKE WESTERN MONEY, WAMPUM WAS VALUABLE BECAUSE IT TOOK HARD WORK TO PRODUCE, NOT BECAUSE IT WAS RARE.

ANOTHER DIFFERENCE WAS THAT WAMPUM BEADS WERE WOVEN INTO BELTS, WHOSE PATTERNS COULD BE MADE TO SPELL OUT MESSAGES.

WHEN TWO NATIONS MADE A TREATY, THEY INSCRIBED ITS TERMS ON SACRED WAMPUM BELTS, WHICH COULD BE USED LATER AS AN AID TO MEMORY.

SO — WHEN THE DUTCH "BOUGHT" MANHATTAN ISLAND FOR $24 WORTH OF GLASS BEADS, THEY WERE PAYING WITH COUNTERFEIT WAMPUM!

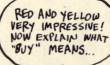

RED AND YELLOW VERY IMPRESSIVE! NOW EXPLAIN WHAT "BUY" MEANS...

··CHAPTER 3··

WHEN A COLONY GROWS UP, WHAT DOES IT DO FOR A LIVING?

LET'S TAKE A COLONIAL TOUR IN THE YEAR

1755

(JUST BEFORE ALL HELL BROKE LOOSE).

START WITH THE SOUTH: GEORGIA, SOUTH CAROLINA, NORTH CAROLINA, VIRGINIA, MARYLAND, DELAWARE... THE LAND OF THE LANDED ARISTOCRACY, THE LAZY PLANTATION ON THE LAZY RIVER... THE LAND OF THE "BIG HOUSE," THE FOX HUNT, THE HORSE RACE, THE GAMBLING DEBT, THE MINT JULEP.

PLANTATION PRODUCTS INCLUDED TOBACCO, INDIGO, JUTE, AND RICE. THE WORK, OF COURSE, WAS DONE BY "SHIFTLESS" SLAVES.

WHEN SLAVERY WAS FIRST INTRODUCED IN THE SOUTH, IT WASN'T EXACTLY LEGAL...

WELL, IT WASN'T ILLEGAL EITHER!

THERE JUST WEREN'T ANY LAWS ON THE BOOKS, AND FOR A LONG TIME, THE SLAVE COLONIES DIDN'T BOTHER TO WRITE ANY.

THIS WAS IN THE GRAND AMERICAN TRADITION OF OPPOSITION TO GOVERNMENT REGULATION, ESPECIALLY WHEN YOU'RE DOING SOMETHING UNSPEAKABLE.

SH!

BUT THEN THE LAWYERS GOT HOLD OF THE QUESTION... THEY BEGAN A LONG, EXPENSIVE ARGUMENT ABOUT WHETHER OR NOT SLAVES WERE REAL ESTATE (!)... SO THE WHITES DECIDED IT WOULD BE CHEAPER IN THE LONG RUN TO PUT SOMETHING IN WRITING.

OTHERWISE, WE'LL ALL END UP AS SLAVES OF THE LAWYERS!

43

THE RESULTING "SLAVE CODES" VARIED FROM ONE COLONY TO THE NEXT, BUT THEY MOSTLY LOOKED LIKE THIS:

IT WAS

ILLEGAL

FOR SLAVES TO CARRY ANY KIND OF WEAPON

FOR A BLACK TO LIFT A HAND AGAINST A WHITE, EVEN IN SELF-DEFENSE

FOR SLAVES TO MARRY

FOR SLAVES TO HAVE FUNERALS

IT WAS

LEGAL

FOR A MASTER TO WORK HIS SLAVES 6 DAYS A WEEK, 15 HOURS A DAY — AND THEN MAKE THEM GROW THEIR OWN FOOD ON SUNDAYS

FOR A MASTER TO PUNISH HIS SLAVES IN ANY WAY HE WANTED, INCLUDING DEATH

MORE ?

SLAVES WEREN'T ALLOWED TO HAVE LIQUOR, OR STUDY READING.

A SLAVE HAD NO RIGHT TO A JURY TRIAL... SLAVE PRISONERS WERE DENIED HEAT IN THEIR CELLS (FOR FEAR THEY'D BURN DOWN THE JAIL).

AND "RACE MIXING" WAS ILLEGAL — WHICH ONLY PROVES THAT NOT ALL THE LAWS WERE ENFORCED 100%!

ISN'T THAT RIGHT, DAD?!

WITH THOUSANDS (LATER MILLIONS) OF SLAVES IN THEIR MIDST, THE WHITE SOUTH WAS NATURALLY NERVOUS ABOUT THE POSSIBILITY OF SLAVE REVOLTS.

HOWDY, GOV'NOR!

"FREEDOM WEARS A CAP WHICH CAN WITHOUT WORDS CALL TOGETHER ALL THOSE WHO LONG TO SHAKE OFF THE FETTERS OF SLAVERY..."
—GOV. SPOTTSWOOD OF VIRGINIA

THE FEAR WAS JUSTIFIED BY MAJOR UPRISINGS IN 1663, 1687, 1712, 1720, 1739, 1741, AND LOADS OF MINOR REVOLTS.

(ALL OF THEM WERE PUT DOWN FEROCIOUSLY.)

PERSONAL UPRISINGS — I.E., RUNAWAYS — WERE SO COMMON THAT NEWSPAPERS HAD STANDARD ILLUSTRATIONS FOR RUNAWAY SLAVE ADS.

NOW APPEARING IN A FREE PRESS!

45

BUT THE MAIN RESTRAINT
ON SLAVE REVOLTS
WAS THE FACT THAT
THE SLAVES ALWAYS
FORMED A MINORITY
OF THE SOUTHERN
POPULATION.

80% OF
SOUTHERN WHITE
FAMILIES NEVER
OWNED A SINGLE
SLAVE !!

BLESSED
ARE THE
POOR, FOR
THEY OUTNUMBER
THE SLAVES!

THIS WAS THE OTHER SIDE OF THE OLD SOUTH: THE
POOR FARMERS, BEHIND THE PLANTATIONS, UP IN THE
HILLS, ON THE FRONTIER, WORKING THE SECOND-BEST
SOIL, LIVING IN PLACES WITH NAMES LIKE PEEDEE,
THE WAXHAWS, AND NINETY-SIX. THEY WERE THE
ONES WHO FACED THE INDIANS, COPED WITH
BANDITS, AND WHO ULTIMATELY WOULD
FIGHT TO DEFEND
THE SLAVE
SYSTEM.

YEW
C'N CALL
IT LOCAL
COLOR...

AH CALLS
IT
DIRT PORE!

COMPLEX
PLACE,
THE SOUTH...

46

NOW ONWARD TO THE
MIDDLE COLONIES
(PENNSYLVANIA, NEW YORK, AND NEW JERSEY). IN LATER YEARS, THESE BECAME THE "SOOT STATES"....

...BUT IN THOSE DAYS, THEY WERE NORTH AMERICA'S BREADBASKET, WHERE FREE FARMERS GREW FAR MORE PEAS, BEANS, AND GRAIN THAN THEY COULD POSSIBLY EAT.

STRANGE IDEA!

OTHER POPULAR WAYS TO MAKE MONEY THERE WERE TRADE, CONSTRUCTION, THE LAW, AND REAL ESTATE SPECULATION.

MEANING: BUYING & SELLING VERMONT!

(THAT LAST SEEMED ESPECIALLY WEIRD TO THE INDIANS, WHO THOUGHT OF THE LAND AS THE MOTHER OF US ALL...)

WHO BUYS AND SELLS HIS OWN MOTHER?

MAKE ME AN OFFER...

47

AND ON TO

NEW ENGLAND,

WITH ITS TIDY VILLAGES, STONY SOIL, THRIFTY INHABITANTS, AND BLUE LAWS.

ALL WORK AND NO PLAY MAKES MORE MONEY IN A DAY!

PURITAN POLITICAL POWER MAY HAVE WANED, BUT THE PURITAN ETHIC REMAINED.

THAT'S WHY NEW ENGLANDERS NAMED THEIR CHILDREN AFTER THE PURITAN VIRTUES, SO THEY COULDN'T FORGET WHAT'S IMPORTANT IN LIFE EVEN IF THEY TRIED.

MEET MY DAUGHTERS, PRUDENCE, HOPE, HONOR, FAITH, MERCY, ASSERTIVENESS, AND BOTTOMLINE.

48

NEW ENGLAND'S WEALTH
WAS IN ITS FORESTS...
THE BIGGEST TREES BECAME
MASTS FOR THE ROYAL NAVY,
AND THE REST WERE
TURNED INTO SHIPS IN
BOSTON, PROVIDENCE, AND
NEWPORT.

THE WHOLE ECONOMY
REVOLVED AROUND
SHIPPING: WAREHOUSING,
BARRELMAKING, ROPE
MANUFACTURE..

⇒ BUT THE
BAY COLONY'S
BIGGEST MANUFACTURING
INDUSTRY WAS
SOMETHING ELSE
AGAIN: IT WAS THE
DISTILLATION OF —

RUM

SHOCKING!

49

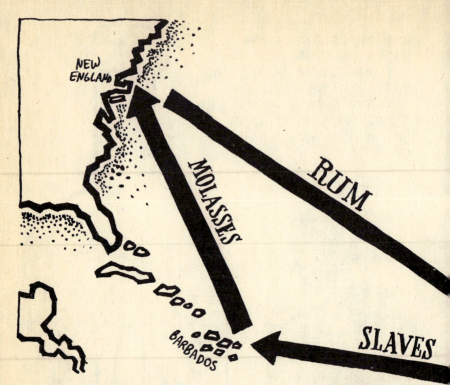

NOT TO WORRY... THE
RUM WASN'T FOR
DRINKING AT HOME... IT
WAS IN REALITY ONE
LEG OF THE FAMOUS

TRIANGULAR TRADE.

HERE'S THE PICTURE:
THE RUM TRAVELS TO AFRICA... IS
TRADED FOR SLAVES... THEY GO TO
THE SUGAR PLANTATIONS OF BARBADOS...
ARE TRADED (AT 1000% MARKUP) FOR
MOLASSES... WHICH GOES TO NEW
ENGLAND... IS DISTILLED INTO RUM...

AND
ROUND
AND
ROUND
AND
ROUND
AND...

50

THE SLAVE SHIPS WERE AN
EXAMPLE OF PURITAN EFFICIENCY
GONE MAD... THEY REALLY
PACKED THEM IN... TRY TO
IMAGINE SPENDING 40 DAYS
CHAINED BELOW DECKS IN
A SPACE 13 INCHES WIDE
AND 18 INCHES HIGH... AND
YOU HAVE THE TRIANGLE'S
DREAD "MIDDLE PASSAGE."

SOME
GEOMETRY
LESSON!

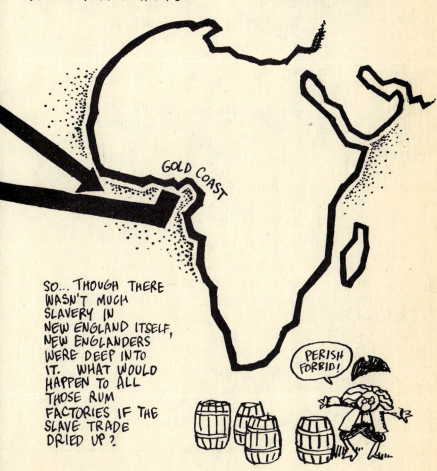

GOLD COAST

SO... THOUGH THERE
WASN'T MUCH
SLAVERY IN
NEW ENGLAND ITSELF,
NEW ENGLANDERS
WERE DEEP INTO
IT. WHAT WOULD
HAPPEN TO ALL
THOSE RUM
FACTORIES IF THE
SLAVE TRADE
DRIED UP?

PERISH
FORBID!

BOSTON "BOTTOMS" CARRIED MORE THAN JUST RUM, SLAVES, AND MOLASSES.

ALSO: BIBLES, CODFISH, BEANS, BEAVER PELTS, DEERSKINS, COWHIDE, TOBACCO, HEMP, INDIGO, TEA, SPICES, ENGLISH GOODS OF ALL KINDS..

(EVEN ICE TO BRITISH SAHIBS IN INDIA!)

SIP!

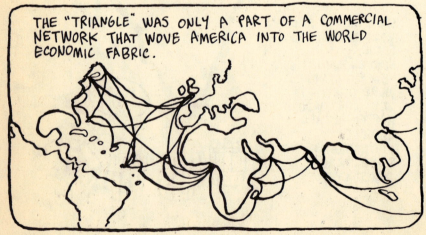

THE "TRIANGLE" WAS ONLY A PART OF A COMMERCIAL NETWORK THAT WOVE AMERICA INTO THE WORLD ECONOMIC FABRIC.

AND THE BOSTON WATERFRONT BUSTLED WITH WAREHOUSES, SHIPPING OFFICES, MARINE SUPPLY HOUSES, EXCHANGES, A CUSTOMS HOUSE (ALWAYS MYSTERIOUSLY UNDERUSED), AND TAVERNS.

WHAT'S THAT? TAVERNS?

SURE... YOU DIDN'T THINK THAT **ALL** THAT RUM LEFT TOWN?

INDEED — IT SEEMED THAT UPRIGHT, UPTIGHT BOSTON HAD DEVELOPED A RAUNCHY UNDERBELLY OF WATERFRONT WORKERS!

HM! NOR'EAST WIND TONIGHT... MUST BE TIME FOR ANOTHER RIOT...

53

YES... RIOTING WAS ONE OF BOSTON'S FAVORITE RECREATIONS! FOR EXAMPLE:

1737: THE "MARKET RIOTS": RIOTERS DISGUISED AS CLERGYMEN (!) DESTROYED MARKET BUILDINGS TO PROTEST GOVERNMENT REGULATION.

1747: "IMPRESSMENT RIOTS": 5000 ANTI-DRAFT PROTESTERS BURNED A BOAT IN THE GOVERNOR'S FRONT YARD.

EVERY NOV. 5: "POPE'S DAY" RIOTS... JUST TO KEEP IN PRACTICE, "NORTH ENDERS" BATTLED "SOUTH ENDERS" IN AN ANNUAL GAME OF "CAPTURE THE POPE."

THIS CONCLUDES OUR COLONIAL TOUR... BUT DON'T WORRY... THERE ARE MORE RIOTS TO COME...

THE COLONIES HAD A LOT IN COMMON: SAME LANGUAGE, SAME KING AND COUNTRY, SAME RELIGION (MORE OR LESS), SAME ENEMIES, EVEN THE SAME SLAVERY... BUT IN THOSE DAYS, BEFORE BARGAIN AIR FARES, TELEVISION, FEDERAL FUNDING, AND KENTUCKY FRIED CHICKEN, THERE WERE ALSO SOME BIG DIFFERENCES, AS THE COLONISTS SAW IT—

THE NEW ENGLANDER IS HALF MAD... HIS IDEA OF A GOOD TIME IS TO PREACH SERMONS 51 WEEKS OF THE YEAR, AND DESTROY BUILDINGS ON THE 52ND... BESIDES, HE LACKS THE REFINEMENT WHICH CAN ONLY COME FROM WIELDING ABSOLUTE POWER OVER A SERVILE CLASS...

THE SOUTHERNER'S RELIGION IS CORRUPT... HIS MORALS ARE LAX... HIS PLANTATIONS ARE CRUEL... HIS WOMEN ARE EASY... HIS LIFE IS... "SHUDDER"- DEEPLY TEMPTING...

NON-PENNSYLVANIANS ARE ALL OBSESSED...

HEY, I'M JEWISH! WHERE CAN I GO BUT RHODE ISLAND?

ANY CHANCE OF UNITING ALL OF THESE? NOT IN 1765!

ZO WHAT HOPPENED?

CHAPTER 4
MIGHTY BEEFS FROM LITTLE BEAVERS GROW

On April, 1754, a Virginia militia company marched westward. Their mission: to protect english trappers and land speculators from the french competition. Their leader: the very young (22 years, 2 months), very tall (6 feet and change), and very honest (99 on a scale of 100) Colonel **GEORGE WASHINGTON.**

YOUNG GEORGE ORDERED HIS MEN TO ATTACK THE FIRST BUNCH OF FRENCH SOLDIERS THEY OUTNUMBERED, KILLING MOST, CAPTURING SOME, AND EARNING THE COLONEL A REPUTATION AS A MAN OF ACTION.

TOO BAD FRANCE AND ENGLAND WERE AT PEACE AT THE TIME...

THE VIRGINIANS QUICKLY HEAPED UP SOME MUD WALLS AND CHRISTENED THEM "FORT NECESSITY."

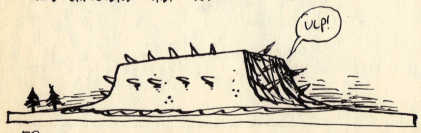

58

WHEN THE REST OF THE
FRENCH ARRIVED, WASHINGTON
BARGAINED HIS PRISONERS
FOR A SAFE MARCH HOME.
THIS WON HIM A
REPUTATION AS A VERY
TOUGH NEGOTIATOR.
(HIS MEN WERE VASTLY
OUTNUMBERED.)

IF HE EVER
LEARNS THE
DIFFERENCE
BETWEEN WAR
AND PEACE, HE
WILL BE TRULY
FORMIDABLE!

THIS INCIDENT IGNITED THE

FRENCH & INDIAN WAR

(WHICH WAS A WAR OF BRITAIN AGAINST THE FRENCH AND
INDIANS, NOT A WAR OF THE FRENCH AND INDIANS
AGAINST EACH OTHER).

WHEN HOSTILITIES BROKE
OUT, WASHINGTON HOPED
FOR A MILITARY PROMOTION.
BUT BRITAIN WANTED
REGULAR ARMY OFFICERS,
NOT 22-YEAR-OLD COLONIALS,
IN COMMAND OF THE TROOPS.
DEMOTED TO MAJOR,
WASHINGTON RAN FOR THE
HOUSE OF BURGESSES,
CARRYING A GREAT
GRUDGE AGAINST LONDON.

THEY'LL
PAY FOR
THIS!

CONTENTS
ONE
GRUDGE

59

AT THIS POINT WE MIGHT WONDER: WHERE DID THOSE FRENCH SOLDIERS COME FROM?

FRANCE, NATURELLEMENT!

WELL, IT ALL GOES BACK TO THE BEAVERS, YOU SEE... FOR MILLIONS OF YEARS, THESE BUSY ANIMALS HAD BEEN EAGERLY GNAWING DOWN TREES, BUILDING DAMS, AND GOING TO LODGE MEETINGS. THEN CAME THE WHITE MAN, AND THE BEAVER STOPPED BEING A CUDDLY RODENT AND BECAME A NATURAL RESOURCE...

WE ARE SUCH STUFF AS HATS ARE MADE OF!

YES, IT GOT SO THAT EUROPEANS COULDN'T LIVE WITHOUT THEIR BEAVER HATS (NOT UNLIKE THE BEAVERS THEMSELVES).

STARTING IN QUEBEC IN 1608, THE FRENCH HAD BUILT A SIZEABLE AMERICAN EMPIRE BASED ON THE FUR TRADE.

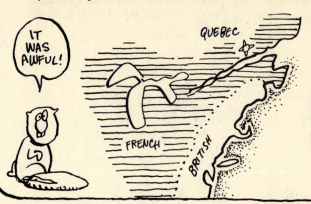

BY 1754, THE BRITISH AND FRENCH EMPIRES WERE RUBBING AGAINST EACH OTHER, CAUSING A RASH ACT.

AFTER WASHINGTON'S FORAY, THE TWO POWERS DECIDED TO FIGHT IT OUT — POSSIBLY THE ONLY WAR EVER FOUGHT OVER HATS.

WHEN IT WAS OVER, IN 1763, BRITAIN HAD WON CANADA AND ITS BEAVERS, AND THE FRENCH WERE OUT OF NORTH AMERICA.

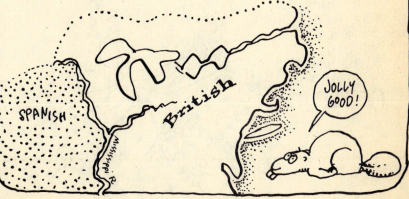

The French and Indian War, like other wars, had a beginning, a middle, and an aftermath. It doubled Britain's national debt and left the colonial economy in the doldrums (a popular rest stop for post-war economies).

Wages are low, but it doesn't matter, because unemployment is high!

But not to worry! Britain had a new (as of 1760), young (born 1738) king, with plenty of fresh ideas and only occasional fits of insanity: GEORGE III.

To REPLENISH
THE TREASURY,
THE KING'S
MINISTERS DREAMED
UP THE
STAMP ACT,
A TAX WHICH
CAME DOWN
ON THE COLONIES
LIKE A
FLAMENCO
PERFORMANCE.

EVERY CONTRACT, NEWSPAPER,
AND GOVERNMENT DOCUMENT
IN THE COLONIES WAS TO
CARRY A GOVERNMENT-ISSUE
STAMP.

ALTHOUGH THE STAMP ACT WAS ONLY A NICKEL-AND-
DIME SORT OF TAX, AMERICA COULD HARDLY AFFORD IT.

BUT THAT WASN'T THE WORST THING ABOUT THE STAMP ACT. THE WORST PART WAS THAT PARLIAMENT HAD PASSED IT WITHOUT THE CONSENT OF THE POTENTIAL TAXEES.* THIS MADE THE STAMP ACT **TAXATION** WITHOUT **REPRESENTATION**, WHICH WOULD HAVE UPSET THE AMERICANS EVEN IF THEIR ECONOMY WASN'T DEPRESSED.

THE COLONISTS, HAVING LITTLE
ELSE TO DO, PROTESTED
AGAINST THE STAMP ACT.
THE VIRGINIA BURGESSES
PASSED RINGING RESOLUTIONS
(THE KIND THAT ALARM
PEOPLE), INTRODUCED BY
PATRICK HENRY,
A FRESHMAN MEMBER
WHO DIDN'T WANT TO
LOSE HIS RIGHTS
BEFORE SOPHOMORE YEAR.

MEANWHILE, THROUGHOUT
THE COLONIES, CITIZENS
CHANTING "LIBERTY
AND PROPERTY" TOOK
LIBERTIES WITH THE
KING'S PROPERTY.
(THESE RIOTS STARTED
IN BOSTON, NATURALLY.)

65

THE PROTESTERS CALLED FOR A TOTAL BOYCOTT OF ALL ENGLISH IMPORTS. FOR EXAMPLE, ANYONE FOUND SUITED IN ENGLISH WOOLENS WOULD BE COATED IN AMERICAN TAR AND FEATHERS.

COLONIAL WOMEN SPUN LIKE MAD—THEIR WHEELS, THAT IS—TO KEEP THEIR FAMILIES IN HOMESPUN, AND OUT OF TAR.

HURRY UP... I'M LATE FOR THE DEMONSTRATION...

JUST EXACTLY AS PLANNED, THE BOYCOTT HIT ENGLISH BUSINESS RIGHT IN THE POCKETBOOK. SOON, THOUSANDS OF SQUEALING, WOUNDED POCKETBOOKS WERE BEGGING PARLIAMENT FOR RELIEF.

IN 1766, THE STAMP ACT WAS REPEALED.

AMERICA CELEBRATED WITH BELLS, FIREWORKS, PARADES, AND REVOLUTIONARY THOUGHTS LIKE THESE!

SOMEHOW FAILING TO GET THE MESSAGE, PARLIAMENT IN 1767 PASSED A NEW TAX, THE "TOWNSHEND DUTIES," ON VARIOUS IMPORTS INTO THE COLONIES. THE HEAD CUSTOMS HOUSE WAS INTELLIGENTLY LOCATED IN BOSTON, WHERE IT WOULD BE SURE TO PROVOKE THE MOST VIOLENCE.

ULP!

AFTER THE INEVITABLE RIOTS, BRITAIN SENT IN THE TROOPS, CALLED "LOBSTERBACKS" AFTER THEIR RED COATS, OR POSSIBLY THEIR CHITINOUS CARAPACES.

WE'LL EAT YAS WIT' DRAWN BUTTER!

FACED WITH A CROWD HURLING ICEBALLS AND EPITHETS, THE SOLDIERS DISCHARGED THEIR DUTY AND THEIR WEAPONS, KILLING FIVE: THE "BOSTON MASSACRE."

THE AUTHORITIES NERVOUSLY REMOVED THE TROOPS... AND SCRAPPED THE TAXES— AGAIN. BUT THEY KEPT ONE LITTLE TAX—ON TEA—JUST TO PROVE THE POINT.

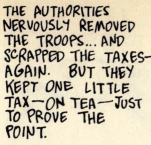

THE POINT BEING—?

THAT NO ONE CAN BOYCOTT CAFFEINE!

SO THE BOSTONIANS, DISGUISED AS INDIANS, DUMPED A SHIPLOAD OF TEA INTO THE DRINK—A TEA PARTY FOR THE FISH.

HOW ABOUT SOME MILK AND SUGAR?

AND A CUP?

HELLO AGAIN!

AS WASTING TEA WAS HIGHLY UN-BRITISH, THE REDCOATS RETURNED TO CLOSE THE PORT UNTIL THE STUFF WAS PAID FOR... AND BOSTON FELL UNUSUALLY QUIET...

THE ONLY SOUND WAS
THE SCRITCH SCRITCH,
SCRITCH OF A QUILL,
AND THE OCCASIONAL
MUFFLED CURSE AS
IT BLOTTED THE
PAGE... THE SOUND
OF THE —

COMMITTEES OF CORRESPONDENCE,

WHICH CORRESPONDED ONLY
WITH EACH OTHER.

ADAMS

HANCOCK

ORIGINALLY THEY
WERE CREATED BY
SAMUEL ADAMS AND
JOHN HANCOCK.
ADAMS WAS THE
BOSTON PROTEST
MOVEMENT'S
MASTERMIND, WHILE
HANCOCK WAS ITS
MASTERCHARGE ACCOUNT.
"SAM ADAMS WRITES
THE LETTERS AND
JOHN HANCOCK PAYS
THE POSTAGE," WENT
THE SAYING. WHO
LICKED THE ENVELOPES
IS ANYBODY'S GUESS.

AT FIRST,
THE COMMITTEES
WERE ONLY IN
MASSACHUSETTS,
BUT THE IDEA
SPREAD TO
ALL THE
COLONIES.
SOON, GROUPS
OF CITIZENS
EVERYWHERE
WERE SWAPPING
REVOLUTIONARY
TIPS, LIKE
BRITAIN'S LATEST
HEINOUS DEEDS,
AND HOW TO
WASH BLOOD
OUT OF
YOUR SHIRT.

"SOAK IN COLD WATER IMMEDIATELY."

CARRIED BY PATRIOT RIDERS
LIKE **PAUL REVERE**, NEWS
OF THE TEA PARTY SPREAD
FAST — AND PROTEST
SWEPT THE COLONIES.

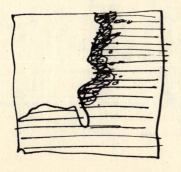

THE BOSTON TEA PARTY WAS
FOLLOWED BY THE GREENWICH (N.J.)
TEA PARTY, THE NEW YORK TEA
PARTY, SEVERAL CHARLESTON (S.C.)
TEA PARTIES, THE PROVIDENCE
(R.I.) TEA PARTY, THE ANNAPOLIS
TEA PARTY... SERIOUS
POLLUTION!!

71

AFTER SOME TIME, THE
COMMITTEES OF
CORRESPONDENCE
DEVELOPED WRITER'S
CRAMP AND DECIDED
TO MEET THEIR
PEN PALS FACE TO
FACE IN
PHILADELPHIA...

NOW I HAVE
SADDLESORES, TOO!

AT A

CONTINENTAL CONGRESS.

ALL THE BIGGIES WERE
THERE: PATRICK HENRY,
GEORGE WASHINGTON, SAM
ADAMS, HIS COUSIN JOHN ADAMS,
JOHN HANCOCK, BENJAMIN
FRANKLIN. IT WAS
OBVIOUSLY A **H**ISTORIC
OCCASION, AND EVERYONE
WAS DEEPLY IMPRESSED, OR
AT LEAST SOMEWHAT
BENT OUT OF SHAPE.

AN HONOR,
I'M SURE!

(ESPECIALLY THRILLED WAS BEN
FRANKLIN, WHO HAD PUSHED
COLONIAL UNION AS EARLY AS
1754 WITH THIS CARTOON.)

ON TOP OF
EVERYTHING
ELSE, HE'S A
CARTOONIST?!!
AWESOME!!

THEY QUICKLY GOT DOWN TO BUSINESS, WHICH CONSISTED OF LOTS OF PARTIES WITH INTERESTING TALK IN THE EVENING, FOLLOWED BY INTERMINABLE SPEECHES DURING THE DAY.

BETWEEN NAPS, THEY DREW UP A **DECLARATION OF RIGHTS** (TOGETHER WITH A **BILL OF WRONGS**), A **PETITION** OR TWO, AND AN **INVOICE** FOR MORE TAR AND FEATHERS.

FINALLY, THEY DECLARED THE CONGRESS A MOST REFRESHING EXPERIENCE AND AGREED TO DO IT AGAIN NEXT YEAR.

MEANWHILE, WITH THE TROOPS STILL IN BOSTON, MASSACHUSETTS TOWNS BEGAN DRILLING THE MINUTEMEN, REVOLUTIONARIES WHO COULD BE READY TO FIGHT IN THE REVOLUTION OF A SECOND HAND.*

THE BRITISH DECIDED TO GET HOLD OF THE PATRIOTS' GUNPOWDER SUPPLY AT CONCORD, OUTSIDE BOSTON. ON THE NIGHT OF APRIL 18, 1775, THEY MARCHED.

WHA~?

THE MINUTEMEN, WARNED BY PAUL REVERE AND OTHERS, MUSTERED ON LEXINGTON GREEN. THE BRITISH OPENED FIRE; THE MINUTEMEN BOLTED; AND SAM ADAMS AND JOHN HANCOCK, AT A NEARBY HOTEL, WOKE UP. IT WAS CHAOS AT 3 A.M.

BY THE TIME THE REDCOATS REACHED CONCORD, THOUSANDS OF PATRIOT FARMERS WERE THERE TO GREET THEM. THIS TIME IT WAS THE BRITISH WHO RETREATED, MARCHING BACK TO BOSTON THROUGH A GAUNTLET OF SNIPERS.

* THIS WAS BEFORE DIGITAL WATCHES.

ADAMS AND HANCOCK HURRIED TO PHILADELPHIA AND THE SECOND CONTINENTAL CONGRESS.

GOOD NEWS! IT'S **WAR!**

OUR GUY GETS THE INSURANCE COMPANY; YOURS GETS THE DOLLAR BILL...

BUT HOW TO GET CONGRESS TO SUPPORT A MASSACHUSETTS BATTLE? IN THE BACK ROOMS, JOHN ADAMS WORKED THE DEAL: A VIRGINIAN WOULD COMMAND THE AMERICAN ARMY, WHILE MASSACHUSETTS' OWN JOHN HANCOCK WOULD BE THE (POWERLESS) PRESIDENT OF CONGRESS.

DO MY EYES DECEIVE ME, OR DO I SEE NEGROES WITH MUSKETS?

AND SO IT WAS THAT A SOUTHERN PLANTER TOOK COMMAND OF A NEW ENGLAND ARMY...

TO WASHINGTON'S EYES, THE REVOLUTIONARY ARMY LOOKED VERY PECULIAR: RACIALLY INTEGRATED, EGALITARIAN, ITS OFFICERS ELECTED BY THE RANK AND FILE.

IT'S AGAINST THE SACRED LAW OF THE PLANTATION!

WASHINGTON IMMEDIATELY ORDERED:

JUST LIKE THE BRITISH ARMY!

- ☆ ALL BLACKS OUT OF THE ARMY
- ☆ NEW OFFICERS TO BE CHOSEN BY THEIR SUPERIORS
- ☆ A RAISE IN OFFICERS' PAY
- ☆ THE USE OF FLOGGING FOR DISCIPLINE

AMID THE HOWLS OF PROTEST, WASHINGTON AGREED TO LET THE BLACKS STAY, BUT REFUSED TO GIVE IN ON THE REST. SO — HALF THE ARMY WENT HOME IN DISGUST.

NOW! LET'S FIGHT THIS REVOLUTION, MEN! MEN? MEN..?

CHAPTER 5

IN WHICH HAPPINESS IS PURSUED, GUN IN HAND

SO—IT WAS
WAR... ON ONE
SIDE, A MIGHTY
EMPIRE, EMBRACING
ENGLAND, SCOTLAND,
IRELAND, AND PARTS OF
GERMANY AND INDIA
(ALTHOUGH NOT ALL
OF THEM RETURNED
THE EMBRACE).

ON THE OTHER —
AN INCREDIBLE
SHRINKING ARMY, A
SELF-APPOINTED
CONGRESS WITHOUT
THE POWER TO TAX
OR DRAFT, AND
NOT EVEN A VERY
CLEAR IDEA WHAT
THEY WERE
FIGHTING FOR...

SOUNDS
GOOD... LET'S
GO WITH
IT!

TOO WEAK TO WIN, CONGRESS COULD ALSO HARDLY AFFORD TO LOSE... NOT WHILE THE REWARD FOR TREASON AGAINST BRITAIN WAS AN INVITATION TO A BARBECUE — OF YOUR OWN INTESTINES.

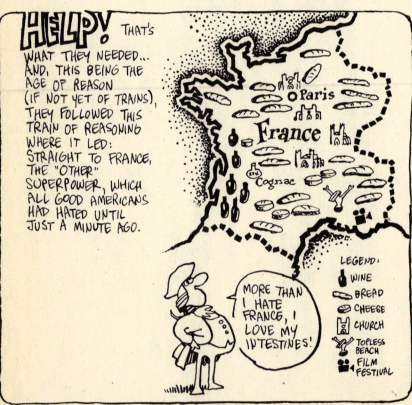

HELP! THAT'S WHAT THEY NEEDED... AND, THIS BEING THE AGE OF REASON (IF NOT YET OF TRAINS), THEY FOLLOWED THIS TRAIN OF REASONING WHERE IT LED: STRAIGHT TO FRANCE, THE "OTHER" SUPERPOWER, WHICH ALL GOOD AMERICANS HAD HATED UNTIL JUST A MINUTE AGO.

France

o Paris

Cognac

MORE THAN I HATE FRANCE, I LOVE MY INTESTINES!

LEGEND:
WINE
BREAD
CHEESE
CHURCH
TOPLESS BEACH
FILM FESTIVAL

BUT—AND THIS WAS A BIG BUT— WHY SHOULD FRANCE HELP THE REBELS, IF THE REBELS' ULTIMATE GOAL WAS TO REMAIN UNITED TO GREAT BRITAIN?

UM... ER... AH... I NEVER THOUGHT OF THAT...

⟹ THAT QUESTION, AMONG OTHERS, WAS RAISED IN THE BEST-SELLING PAMPHLET

"COMMON SENSE,"

WHICH APPEARED IN EARLY 1776. IT CALLED FOR A COMPLETE BREAK WITH ENGLAND.

UP TO THAT POINT, CONGRESS HAD BEEN LOUDLY PROCLAIMING LOYALTY TO KING GEORGE... INDEPENDENCE WAS A GOAL OF ONLY THE WILDEST RADICALS... BUT "COMMON SENSE" CHANGED ALL THAT!

IT'S COMMON SENSE!

AS PUBLIC OPINION SWUNG AROUND, THE RADICALS SEIZED THE INITIATIVE. BY JUNE, 1776, CONGRESS HAD VOTED IN FAVOR OF INDEPENDENCE!!

THE TASK OF WRITING THE DECLARATION OF INDEPENDENCE FELL TO **THOMAS JEFFERSON,** A VIRGINIA CONGRESSMAN WITH A POSITIVE PASSION FOR HUMAN LIBERTY, AS LONG AS THEY WEREN'T HIS HUMANS...

GOSH!

GEE

IF PATRICK HENRY WAS THE REVOLUTION'S GREATEST ORATOR, AND SAM ADAMS THE PREMIER PROTESTER, THEN JEFFERSON WAS THE SUPREME PROSE STYLIST AND POLITICAL VISIONARY.

BEFORE JEFFERSON, THE MOVEMENT'S SLOGAN HAD BEEN "LIBERTY AND PROPERTY..."

IS LIBERTY ANYTHING BESIDES TAX EVASION?

BUT T.J. WANTED TO FOUND THE NEW NATION ON SOMETHING A LITTLE LESS CRASS...

THIS SUBSTITUTE SPRANG TO MIND:

CALL THIS "JEFFERSON'S TIME BOMB!"

"WE HOLD THESE TRUTHS TO BE SELF-EVIDENT, THAT ALL MEN ARE CREATED EQUAL, THAT THEY ARE ENDOWED BY THEIR CREATOR WITH CERTAIN UNALIENABLE RIGHTS, THAT AMONG THESE ARE LIFE, LIBERTY, AND THE PURSUIT OF HAPPINESS..."

NICE...

JEFFERSON'S WORDS WERE
LESS A DESCRIPTION OF
REALITY IN 1776 THAN
A PROMISE FOR THE
FUTURE — THAT EVENTUALLY
EVERYONE WOULD GAIN
EQUAL POLITICAL RIGHTS,
REGARDLESS OF RACE, SEX,
OR INCOME.

O, THE PROMISES OF WHITE FOLKS!

THE DECLARATION ALSO
ANNOUNCED THE PEOPLE'S RIGHT
TO CHOOSE ITS OWN
GOVERNMENT, AN IDEA THAT
HAD BEEN IN THE AIR FOR A
WHILE, BUT HADN'T TOUCHED
GROUND UNTIL NOW.

LOCKE
ROUSSEAU

THE REST
OF THE
PAPER
IS AN
(INFLATED)
LIST OF THE
CRIMES OF
KING GEORGE,
WHO WAS
MADE TO
SOUND A BIT
LIKE A

Giant life like karate practice dummy

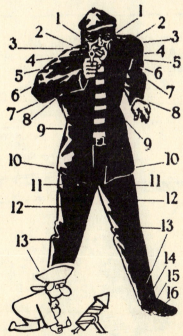

CONGRESS
ACCEPTED THE
DECLARATION OF
INDEPENDENCE
ON THE FOURTH
OF JULY AND
WASTED A
QUANTITY OF
PRECIOUS GUN-
POWDER IN A
FIREWORKS SHOW.

MINDFUL THAT NO NATION IS COMPLETE WITHOUT TRAPPINGS, CONGRESS QUICKLY ADOPTED A FLAG (RED, WHITE, & BLUE), AN ARMY UNIFORM (BROWN), A BIRD (BALD), ARTICLES OF CONFEDERATION (CLUMSY), AND A (ALMOST AS CLUMSY AS THE ARTICLES OF CONFEDERATION):

THE UNITED STATES OF AMERICA

THIS IS A COUNTRY'S NAME?

THIS STARTED A TREND IN NATIONAL NAMES. NOW THAT AN INFINITE VARIETY OF GOVERNMENTS WAS AVAILABLE, INSTEAD OF JUST KINGDOMS, A NAME HAD TO DESCRIBE WHAT IT WAS, OR, ON OCCASION, WHAT IT WASN'T.

PEOPLE'S FEDERATED SOCIALIST REPUBLIC AND DEBATING SOCIETY OF (CONT'D NEXT SIGN)

PRETTY SOON "THE KINGDOM OF GOD" WILL BE "THE ANGELS' REPUBLIC OF HEAVEN..."

LADEN WITH THE NEW NATIONAL TRAPPINGS, BENJAMIN FRANKLIN SAILED FOR FRANCE TO NEGOTIATE FOR AID. HE WORE A BEAVER HAT TO REMIND THE FRENCH OF WHAT COULD BE THEIRS AGAIN, IF THEY PLAYED ALONG...

WHILE THE FRENCH ARISTOCRATS FELL IN LOVE WITH THE AMERICAN, THEY WERE NERVOUS ABOUT HIS GOVERNMENT. AFTER ALL, IT HAD NO KING —AN UNHEARD-OF ARRANGEMENT. FRANKLIN TRIED TO CONVINCE THEM THAT ENGLAND WAS MORE DANGEROUS THAN DEMOCRACY.

THIS PLOY SEEMED TO WORK, AND FRANCE BEGAN FUNNELING COVERT AID TO THE U.S. THROUGH DUMMY CORPORATIONS.

(90% OF U.S. GUNPOWDER CAME FROM FRANCE.)

MEANWHILE, BACK AT THE FRONT, THE WAR HAD BEGUN
WELL AND GOTTEN WORSE.
IN MARCH, 1776,
THE BRITISH, FACED
WITH WASHINGTON'S
CANNON (DRAWN THERE
FROM AFAR BY
HEROIC OXEN)* LEFT
BOSTON FOR NEW YORK
AND A PITCHED
BATTLE. THE AMERICANS,
WHO USUALLY PITCHED
NOTHING HARDER
THAN HAY, FLED IN THE
DIRECTION OF
PHILADELPHIA, GUIDED
BY THE HOWLS OF
CONGRESS.

THE FIRST—UNSUNG AND (UNTIL NOW)-UNPAINTED-CROSSING
OF THE DELAWARE WAS STRICTLY IN REVERSE.

THE SECOND CROSSING WAS A SNEAK ATTACK ON CHRISTMAS
NIGHT, SURPRISING THE ENEMY WHILE THEY WERE STILL
OPENING THEIR PRESENTS. IT LOOKED SOMETHING LIKE THIS:

* THE OXEN WERE LED BY 250-LB HENRY ("OX") KNOX, WHO INSPIRED THE
ANIMALS BY RESEMBLING THEM.

AS 1777 DRAGGED ON, WASHINGTON FAILED TO STOP THE BRITISH FROM TAKING PHILADELPHIA, WHILE THE BRITISH FAILED TO STOP CONGRESS FROM TAKING TO THE HILLS.

SAVE THE PAPERWORK!

CAN'T SEE A BLOODY THING!

WASHINGTON & CO. WENT OFF TO STARVE AT VALLEY FORGE, A DARK HOUR, BRIGHTENED ONLY BY BRITAIN'S INCREDIBLE DIMNESS IN NOT TAKING ADVANTAGE OF THE SITUATION.

AT THE SAME TIME, 7000 EXTRA REDCOATS WERE TRYING TO HURRY SOUTH FROM CANADA. SLOWED BY AMERICAN GUERRILLAS, WHO MADE THEM FEEL LIKE A BUNCH OF CHUMPS, THE ENTIRE INVADING ARMY SURRENDERED AFTER THE BATTLE OF SARATOGA, WHICH MADE THEM FEEL EVEN LOWER, PERHAPS LIKE BABOONS. IT WAS A TURNING POINT IN THE EVOLUTION OF THE REVOLUTION.

WE'RE EVOLVING BACKWARD...

85

WHY A TURNING POINT? BECAUSE SARATOGA SO THRILLED KING **LOUIS** THAT HE LOST HIS HEAD AND MADE AN OPEN ALLIANCE WITH THE DANGEROUSLY DEMOCRATIC U.S.A.

I SMELL THE BLOOD OF AN ENGLISHMAN!

INSTEAD OF COVERT AID, AMERICA NOW HAD FRENCH TROOPS!

HEY, LOUIE! YOU WANT BEAVER CHAPEAU?

BY THIS POINT, A BILATERAL BATTLE HAD ESCALATED INTO A WAR WITH SIX DIFFERENT SIDES...

PATRIOTS:

WHITES & FREE BLACKS, FIRED BY DEMOCRATIC RHETORIC, FOUGHT FOR A SIMPLE GOAL:

BRITISH:

THEY ONLY WANTED TO KEEP THEIR COLONIES, BUT COULDN'T QUITE SEE SEE HOW...

TORIES:

AMERICANS LOYAL TO THE CROWN, THEY HAD ONLY WANTED PEACE & QUIET & LAW & ORDER. NOW THEY WANTED REVENGE.

SLAVES:

MASTER'S FIGHT TO GET OUT FROM UNDER ENGLAND LOOKED LIKE A GOOD OPPORTUNITY TO GET OUT FROM UNDER MASTER.

INDIANS:

MOST SIDED WITH ENGLAND, AS THEY HAD HEARD WHAT THE PATRIOTS WERE FIGHTING FOR.

FRANCE:

THE FRENCH WERE TRYING TO DESTROY THE "EVIL EMPIRE," I.E., ENGLAND.

WITH SO MANY SIDES FIGHTING IN ONE PLACE, EVENTS
SQUEEZED TOGETHER: BATTLES, RIOTS, INFLATION, STRIKES,
A DOG PAPERED WITH DEVALUED MONEY...

WORTH?

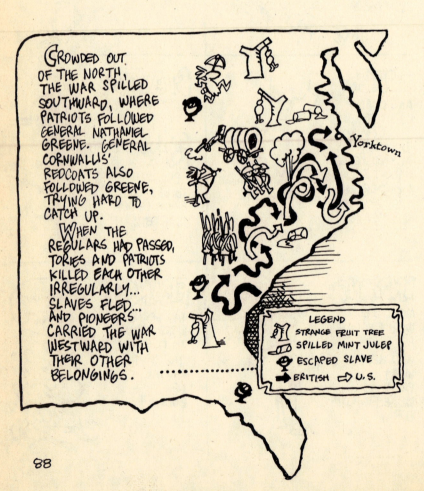

CROWDED OUT
OF THE NORTH,
THE WAR SPILLED
SOUTHWARD, WHERE
PATRIOTS FOLLOWED
GENERAL NATHANIEL
GREENE. GENERAL
CORNWALLIS'
REDCOATS ALSO
FOLLOWED GREENE,
TRYING HARD TO
CATCH UP.

WHEN THE
REGULARS HAD PASSED,
TORIES AND PATRIOTS
KILLED EACH OTHER
IRREGULARLY...
SLAVES FLED...
AND PIONEERS
CARRIED THE WAR
WESTWARD WITH
THEIR OTHER
BELONGINGS.

Yorktown

LEGEND
STRANGE FRUIT TREE
SPILLED MINT JULEP
ESCAPED SLAVE
BRITISH ▷ U.S.

AFTER MARCHING IN LOOPS, CORNWALLIS DIZZILY RESTED AT YORKTOWN, VIRGINIA. WASHINGTON'S ARMY (½ FRENCH, ½ AMERICAN) SUDDENLY APPEARED, AND THE FRENCH NAVY DELIVERED THE **COUP** WHICH IMMORTALIZED THE NAME OF ITS ADMIRAL **DE GRASSE**.

THE BRITISH SURRENDERED (THOUGH CORNWALLIS HIMSELF WAS TOO DISORIENTED TO ATTEND THE CEREMONY). UNLIKE SARATOGA, THIS WAS NOT A TURNING POINT BUT AN EXCLAMATION POINT, OR JUST A POINT, AS IN PERIOD.

AT LEAST THERE'S STILL INDIA...

AFTER YORKTOWN, BRITAIN AND THE U.S.A. HELD PEACE TALKS WHICH PRODUCED THE **TREATY** OF **PARIS** IN 1783.

ENGLAND KEPT CANADA, WHICH TURNED OUT TO BE A **GOOD THING**, ESPECIALLY IF YOU WERE LOYAL TO ENGLAND, AN ESCAPED SLAVE, OR AGAINST THE VIETNAM WAR. SEVERAL CARIBBEAN PARADISES ALSO REMAINED BRITISH, SO THAT NEW YORKERS WOULD HAVE SOMEPLACE FOREIGN TO FLY IN THE WINTER.

THE **U.S.A.** GOT WHAT IT WANTED, WHICH WAS EVERYTHING.

ALL THAT FOR US?

WHAT DO YOU MEAN, "US"?

FRANCE WAS CUT OUT OF THE DEAL COMPLETELY, ALTHOUGH KING LOUIS EVENTUALLY GOT MORE THAN HE BARGAINED FOR, OR LESS.

HOW WAS I TO KNOW THAT REVOLUTION IS CONTAGIOUS?

AMERICAN **TORIES** HAD A CHOICE: STAY, AND WATCH THEIR PROPERTY PILLAGED BY PATRIOTS, OR GO TO CANADA, WHERE THEY WOULDN'T HAVE TO WATCH. MOST OF THEM STAYED.

I HAD TO STAY: THEY STOLE MY SUITCASE!

ABOUT 60,000 **SLAVES** ESCAPED, TRAVELING AMAZING ODYSSEYS TO CANADA, FLORIDA, AFRICA, JAMAICA, ETC... ANOTHER 700,000 SLAVES REMAINED SLAVES, TO HELP CARRY THIS VOLUME TO ITS CONCLUSION.

AND THEY CALL IT "LIGHT READING."

AND THE **INDIANS** GOT—WELL, YOU KNOW WHAT THE INDIANS GOT.

COWBOYS...

92

·CHAPTER 6·

SHOES, MYTAS, THE CONSTITUTION, ETC.

ND SO IT BEGAN... THE AMERICAN DREAM... AND THE AMERICAN MYTH... AND WHAT COULD BE MORE MYTHIC — OR MORE AMERICAN — THAN THE WAGON TRAIN ??

ACTUALLY, THE WAGON TRAINS OF
THE 1780's WERE PRETTY SMALL...
SMALL BUT MYTHIC... AT LEAST,
THE FRONT END WAS MYTHIC, WITH
ITS WAGONMASTERS, SCOUTS, AND
PIONEER FAMILIES HOPING TO
CARVE OUT A NEW LIFE BEFORE
IT CARVED THEM FIRST.

BUT THE SLAVE CARAVAN, OR SOUL TRAIN,
AT THE REAR, WAS LEFT OUT OF THE
FORWARD-LOOKING AMERICAN MYTH.
THE SLAVES BELONGED TO GENTLEMEN*
PIONEERS, WHOSE VISION OF TENNESSEE
AND KENTUCKY WAS IDENTICAL TO
VIRGINIA OR CAROLINA, ONLY A LITTLE
TO THE LEFT, ON THE MAP, THAT IS.

* SO-CALLED BECAUSE PEOPLE TREATED THEM GENTLY, NOT VICE VERSA

95

WHERE ARE WE HEADING, AS A NATION, I MEAN?

THE SPREAD OF SLAVERY WAS ALARMING, AND NOT ONLY TO THE SLAVES. A NUMBER OF WHITES HAD ALSO NOTICED SOMETHING IN THE DECLARATION OF INDEPENDENCE ABOUT "ALL MEN" HAVING A RIGHT TO LIBERTY.

I DON'T *THINK* IT SAYS "EXCEPT NEGROES..."

ANTI-SLAVERY WHITES FAILED REPEATEDLY TO HALT ITS EXPANSION. IN 1784, WHEN CONGRESS CONSIDERED A BAN ON SLAVERY IN THE WEST, THE MEASURE LOST BY A SINGLE VOTE, AND THE RELENTLESS WESTERN CLANK CONTINUED.

HEY, DID YOU HEAR THE ONE ABOUT THE NATION CONCEIVED IN LIBERTY?

IF IT WAS ANY CONSOLATION, CONTROLLING SLAVERY WASN'T THE GOVERNMENT'S ONLY PROBLEM. FOR EXAMPLE, THERE WAS ALSO THE PROBLEM OF THE SHOES — 30,000 PAIRS OF IMPORTED SHOES, TO BE EXACT, DUMPED ON THE NEW YORK MARKET AT ROCK-BOTTOM PRICES.

THIS WAS CONSIDERED (U)NFAIR (C)OMPETITION BY NEW YORK'S SHOEMAKERS, WHO BELIEVED IN AMERICAN SHOES, WITH LEATHER BOTTOMS AND PRICES TO MATCH.

ISN'T THAT WHAT THE REVOLUTION WAS ABOUT?

BUT ALAS... CONGRESS, IN ITS WISDOM, HAD FORGOTTEN TO GIVE ITSELF THE POWER TO REGULATE IMPORTS... AND SO THE COBBLERS HAD NO PIE...

TIME TO BREAK OUT THE TAR AND FEATHERS AGAIN...

THEN THERE WAS THE DEBT PROBLEM, THE PROBLEM BEING
THAT EVERYONE WAS IN IT, ESPECIALLY FARMERS AND
THE GOVERNMENT. (CONGRESS HAD CLEVERLY FAILED TO GIVE
ITSELF THE POWER TO COLLECT TAXES.) AFTER THE REVOLUTION,
DEBT-RIDDEN FARMERS FOUND THEMSELVES FACING EVICTION.

THE FARMERS,
WHO WERE
VETERANS OF
THE REVOLUTION,
WENT FOR THEIR
MUSKETS.

WHAT EVER HAPPENED TO LIBERTY **AND** PROPERTY?

THE BANKERS WERE HORRIFIED! THEY BELIEVED THAT GOVERNMENTS EXIST TO HELP COLLECT LOAN PAYMENTS, AND WHO'S TO SAY THEY WERE WRONG?

WHEN ARMED FARMERS RESISTED, AS IN SHAYS' REBELLION (1786), BIG WEALTH DECIDED THAT THE REVOLUTION HAD GONE TOO FAR...

THEY'RE UNCHECKED! I'M UNBALANCED!

"TOO MUCH DEMOCRACY," THEY GRUMBLED, NOTING THAT A FORMER SHOEMAKER WAS NOW LIEUTENANT GOVERNOR OF NEW YORK. WHAT WAS NEXT?

PERMANENT HOLES IN MY SOLES?

99

IN 1787, THE "BETTER CLASS" OF CITIZENS, WHICH INCLUDED BANKERS, BUSINESSMEN, SLAVE OWNERS, AND, FOR SOME REASON, LAWYERS, DECIDED TO DO SOMETHING.

IF THE FARMERS CAN TAKE THE LAW INTO THEIR OWN HANDS, BY GOD WE'LL TAKE THE WHOLE ⚡☉# GOVERNMENT!

ARTICLES OF CONFEDERATION

THEY CONVENED IN PHILADELPHIA TO CONSIDER CHANGES IN THE PLAN OF GOVERNMENT. AT THE TIME, THE U.S.A. WAS OPERATING, IF YOU CAN CALL IT THAT, UNDER THE ARTICLES OF CONFEDERATION, THE WONDERFUL DOCUMENT THAT PREVENTED CONGRESS FROM COLLECTING TAXES OR REGULATING COMMERCE.

THE VERY FIRST CHANGE WAS TO THROW OUT THE ARTICLES OF CONFEDERATION ENTIRELY.

ALTHOUGH VERY FEW OF THEM WERE IN THE CONSTRUCTION BUSINESS, THE CONSTITUTION-WRITERS ARE KNOWN AS THE "FRAMERS." THEY INCLUDED:

GEORGE WASHINGTON, FROM THE $1 BILL...

ALEXANDER HAMILTON, FROM THE TEN...

BEN FRANKLIN, FROM THE HUNDRED.

(JEFFERSON, WHO WAS ABSENT, LATER APPEARED ON THE $2 BILL, WHICH NOBODY USED.)

THE FRAMERS' PROBLEM: THEY BELIEVED IN REPUBLICAN GOVERNMENT (NO ONE TRUSTED ANYONE ELSE TO BE KING), BUT THEY DIDN'T BELIEVE IN "POPULAR" GOVERNMENT (TOO MUCH POWER FOR THE POOR). THEY BELIEVED IN PRIVATE WEALTH, BUT THEY KNEW HOW THE RICH COULD HOG POWER AT PUBLIC COST...

THEREFORE: A "MIXED" GOVERNMENT, WITH A POPULAR ELEMENT, BUT ENOUGH CLOUT FOR THE RICH TO SAVE THEM THE BOTHER OF OVERHAULING IT AGAIN...

WHAT A JOB!

AMERICANS, WHO BY NOW HAD THE PRACTICAL EQUIVALENT OF 3 MILLION PH.D.'S IN POLITICAL SCIENCE, ALL KNEW WHAT THE MOST RESPONSIVE AND ACCOUNTABLE KIND OF GOVERNMENT WAS: A LEGISLATURE, ELECTED BY THE PEOPLE,* AND RE-ELECTED OFTEN, TO PRESERVE FRESHNESS.

JUST LIKE CONGRESS, UNDER THE ARTICLES OF CONFEDERATION!

THE FRAMERS KEPT ONE OF THESE IN THEIR PLAN, BUT THEY MAGICALLY SHRANK IT DOWN TO ONE HALF OF ONE OF THREE BRANCHES OF GOVERNMENT. THIS IS THE HOUSE OF REPRESENTATIVES, OR "LOWER" HOUSE.

THE CHAMBER OF HORRORS!

*BEARING IN MIND THAT POOR, BLACK, AND FEMALE PEOPLE HADN'T BEEN DISCOVERED YET.

102

ON TOP OF THE HOUSE WERE HEAPED THE SENATE, THE EXECUTIVE, AND THE JUDICIARY. THESE WERE DESIGNED TO IMPEDE AND FRUSTRATE EACH OTHER, THE IDEA BEING TO PREVENT ANY ONE BRANCH FROM BECOMING TOO POWERFUL. THIS DESIGN, WHICH SUCCEEDED, IS CALLED THE SYSTEM OF CHECKS AND BALANCES.

BECAUSE IT'S HARD TO KEEP YOUR BALANCE WHEN YOU'RE BEING CHECKED!

THE NEW GOVERNMENT WAS GIVEN POWERS TO MATCH ITS BULK: THE POWER TO TAX, TO REGULATE TRADE, TO MAKE WAR, TO RAISE A BUREAUCRACY, ETC...

HM! SOUNDS LIKE THE BRITISH GOVERNMENT...

THAT SOLVED THE PROBLEMS OF TAXES, DEBT, POWER, "EXCESS" DEMOCRACY, COMMERCE — EVERY PROBLEM BUT ONE...THE ONE THAT COULD ONLY BE DESCRIBED IN CIRCUMLOCUTIONS,* AS IT WAS TOO EMBARRASSING TO SAY IN PUBLIC, IN A REPUBLIC...

THE 5 SOUTHERN STATES, A MINORITY, WANTED GUARANTEES THAT THE NORTHERN MAJORITY WOULDN'T TAMPER WITH SLAVERY. WHENEVER A NORTHERN DELEGATE SUGGESTED THAT BLACKS HAD RIGHTS, TOO, SOUTH CAROLINA WOULD THREATEN TO GO HOME.

WE'LL START OUR OWN DAMN COUNTRY!

SL— SL— SL—

THE NORTH, ANXIOUS TO AVOID CIVIL WAR (AT LEAST FOR THE TIME BEING), AGREED TO MAKE SOME CONCESSIONS TO PREVENT SECESSION.

OH, COME ON, SAY IT!

WELL, SHET MY MOUTH!

*SEE NEXT PAGE.

HERE WAS THE DEAL:

SOUTHERN WHITES WERE GIVEN OVER-REPRESENTATION IN THE HOUSE, BY ALLOWING 3/5 OF THE "OTHER PERSONS" * TO BE COUNTED ON TOP OF THE WHITE POPULATION, EVEN THOUGH THEY WERE REALLY UNDERNEATH IT.

IN RETURN, SOUTHERNERS IN CONGRESS AGREED TO A BAN ON SLAVERY IN THE FUTURE STATES NORTH OF THE OHIO RIVER, PROVIDED THAT THE NUMBER OF STATES THERE WAS HELD TO THREE — OHIO, INDIANA, ILLINOIS — THUS LIMITING NORTHERN INFLUENCE IN THE SENATE.

AND...

THE NORTH PROMISED TO RETURN ANY "PERSON HELD TO SERVICE OR LABOR" * WHO ESCAPED.

THE SLAVE TRADE, OR "IMPORTATION OF SUCH PERSONS AS ANY OF THE STATES SHALL THINK PROPER TO ADMIT," * WOULD CONTINUE UNTIL AT LEAST 1808.

...THAT WAS THE COMPROMISE OF 1787.

*SEE PREVIOUS FOOTNOTE.

BUT DRAFTING A CONSTITUTION WASN'T ENOUGH. IT ALSO HAD TO BE AIRED. WHEN THE PUBLIC CAUGHT WIND OF ITS CONTENTS, A STORMY DEBATE BLEW UP, WITH BOTH SIDES THUNDERING INSULTS AT EACH OTHER.

OPPONENTS BLASTED THE PLAN AS OVER-CENTRALIZED AND ANTI-DEMOCRATIC, WHILE PROPONENTS MADE BREEZY DENIALS.

THE "ANTIS" ALSO NOTICED A FEW THINGS MISSING FROM THE DOCUMENT: LIKE ANYTHING ABOUT FREEDOM OF SPEECH, RELIGION, AND THE PRESS... THE RIGHT TO BEAR ARMS, DUE PROCESS, A SPEEDY TRIAL, ETC., ETC, ETC... THE EMBARRASSED FRAMERS PROMISED TO ADD A BILL OF RIGHTS, OR, IN MORE BIBLICAL LANGUAGE, THE TEN AMENDMENTS.

A MERE OVERSIGHT!

AFTER MANY MONTHS OF MUD-SLINGING, GUN-WAVING, POLITICAL SKULL-DIGGERY AND -DUGGERY, AND OCCASIONAL HONEST DEBATE, THE CONSTITUTION WAS ADOPTED, AND EVERYONE IMMEDIATELY FELL TO WORSHIPPING IT, WHICH IS HOW IT'S BEEN EVER SINCE, ALMOST.

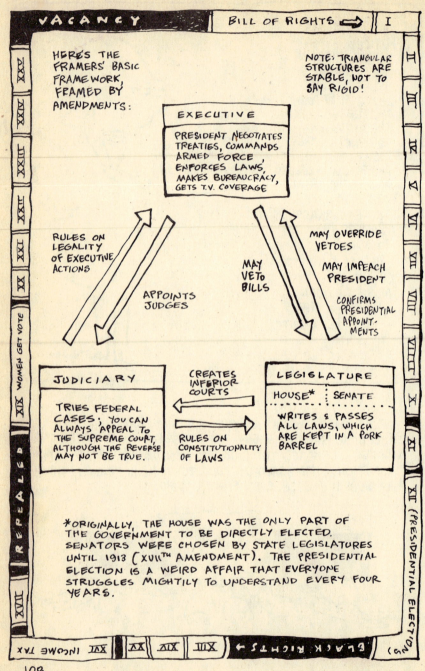

HERE'S THE FRAMERS' BASIC FRAMEWORK, FRAMED BY AMENDMENTS:

NOTE: TRIANGULAR STRUCTURES ARE STABLE, NOT TO SAY RIGID!

EXECUTIVE

PRESIDENT NEGOTIATES TREATIES, COMMANDS ARMED FORCE, ENFORCES LAWS, MAKES BUREAUCRACY, GETS T.V. COVERAGE

RULES ON LEGALITY OF EXECUTIVE ACTIONS

MAY OVERRIDE VETOES

MAY IMPEACH PRESIDENT

CONFIRMS PRESIDENTIAL APPOINTMENTS

MAY VETO BILLS

APPOINTS JUDGES

JUDICIARY

TRIES FEDERAL CASES; YOU CAN ALWAYS APPEAL TO THE SUPREME COURT, ALTHOUGH THE REVERSE MAY NOT BE TRUE.

CREATES INFERIOR COURTS

RULES ON CONSTITUTIONALITY OF LAWS

LEGISLATURE

HOUSE* : SENATE

WRITES & PASSES ALL LAWS, WHICH ARE KEPT IN A PORK BARREL

*ORIGINALLY, THE HOUSE WAS THE ONLY PART OF THE GOVERNMENT TO BE DIRECTLY ELECTED. SENATORS WERE CHOSEN BY STATE LEGISLATURES UNTIL 1913 (XVIITH AMENDMENT). THE PRESIDENTIAL ELECTION IS A WEIRD AFFAIR THAT EVERYONE STRUGGLES MIGHTILY TO UNDERSTAND EVERY FOUR YEARS.

XXV · XXIV · XXIII · XXII · XXI · XX · XIX WOMEN GET VOTE · REPEALED · XVIII

II · III · IV · V · VI · VII · VIII · IX · X · XI · XII (PRESIDENTIAL ELECTIONS)

XVII INCOME TAX · XVI · XV · XIV · XIII · ⟵ BLACK RIGHTS ⟶

✫ CHAPTER 7 ✫

MR. JEFFERSON THROWS A PARTY

GEORGE WASHINGTON WAS UNANIMOUSLY ELECTED TO BE THE FIRST PRESIDENT UNDER THE NEW CONSTITUTION.

CONGRESS IMMEDIATELY DEBATED FOR THREE WEEKS WHETHER TO ADDRESS HIM AS "MR. PRESIDENT" OR "YOUR MAJESTY."

THIS SPLIT— BETWEEN THOSE WHO WANTED THEIR GOVERNMENT PLAIN VS. THOSE WHO WANTED IT POMPOUS— QUICKLY SPILLED OVER INTO OTHER AREAS.

THE NEXT FIGHT
STARTED WITH A
PROVOCATIVE PROPOSAL
FROM TREASURY
SECRETARY
ALEXANDER
HAMILTON.

LET'S
GIVE THE
COUNTRY
TO THE
RICH!

DURING THE REVOLUTION, SAID
HAMILTON, THE STATE
GOVERNMENTS HAD BORROWED
HEAVILY — AND NEVER
REPAID THEIR DEBTS. NOW,
VAST QUANTITIES OF
STATE-ISSUED I.O.U.'S WERE
FLOATING AROUND ... BOUGHT,
SOLD, AND COLLECTED, SOMETHING
LIKE BASEBALL CARDS. *

I'LL GIVE
YOU TWO
MARYLANDS
FOR A STAN
MUSIAL...

HAMILTON'S PLAN WAS
FOR THE FEDERAL
GOVERNMENT TO
REPAY EVERY I.O.U.
AT FACE VALUE — A
HUGE WINDFALL FOR
THE HOLDERS.

GOOD
IDEA,
ALEX!

*EXCEPT THAT BASEBALL CARDS SOMETIMES RISE IN VALUE.

SECRETARY OF STATE THOMAS JEFFERSON ACCUSED HAMILTON OF SCHEMING TO MORTGAGE THE NATION TO THE EASTERN MONEY ESTABLISHMENT, AT TAXPAYER EXPENSE.

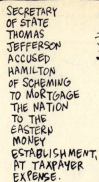

"THE MORE DEBT HAMILTON COULD RAKE UP, THE MORE PLUNDER FOR HIS MERCENARIES. THIS MONEY, WHETHER WISELY OR FOOLISHLY SPENT, WAS PRETENDED TO HAVE BEEN SPENT FOR GENERAL PURPOSES, AND OUGHT, THEREFORE, TO BE PAID FROM THE GENERAL PURSE."

HAMILTON RETORTED THAT A BIG NATIONAL DEBT WAS A **GOOD THING,** BECAUSE THE RICH, HOPING TO BE REPAID, WILL SUPPORT STRONG GOVERNMENT.

MOMMY

JEFFERSON REPLIED THAT A BIG DEBT CAUSES THE GOVERNMENT TO FAVOR THE RICH, WHO LOAN IT MONEY, AND TO CRUSH THE POOR, WHO HAVE TO PAY IT OFF.

JEFFERSON SNEERED THAT HAMILTON WAS TRYING TO BUY POLITICAL SUPPORT... HAMILTON SNARLED THAT HE SAW NOTHING WRONG WITH THAT... ENGLAND HAD BEEN RUNNING THAT WAY FOR GENERATIONS...

MONARCHIST!

FOOL! REDHEAD!

THIS FIGHT ENDED WITH A STRANGE COMPROMISE: JEFFERSON DROPPED HIS OPPOSITION TO THE TREASURY PLAN, WHILE HAMILTON BACKED JEFFERSON'S PET PROJECT, A NATIONAL CAPITAL IN THE SOUTH! AND THAT'S WHY WASHINGTON, D.C., WAS BUILT ON THE BANKS OF THE POTOMAC!

COURTESY OF THE BANKS OF N.Y.!

AH... BUT THERE WAS STILL THE MATTER OF THE

FRENCH REVOLUTION!

INSPIRED BY THE
AMERICANS, THE
FRENCH PEOPLE HAD
RISEN UP AND GIVEN
THEIR KING AN
OPERATION WHICH MADE
IT NECESSARY TO
DECLARE A REPUBLIC.

JEFFERSON, WHO FELT LIKE ITS AMERICAN GODFATHER, WAS
ALL FOR THE FRENCH REVOLUTION. HAMILTON, WHO MORE
ADMIRED ENGLAND, WHERE PATRIOTISM AND PECUNIARY
SELF-INTEREST WERE BLENDED TO THE POINT THAT NO
ONE COULD TELL THE DIFFERENCE,* WAS SUSPICIOUS OF
ANYTHING BASED PURELY ON PRINCIPLES.

*ONLY AT THAT TIME, NO DOUBT

HAMILTON ATTACKED JEFFERSON IN THE PRESS... JEFFERSON SECRETLY STARTED HIS OWN NEWSPAPER TO SAVAGE HAMILTON AND CELEBRATE HIMSELF...

THE COMMON PEOPLE, WITH JEFFERSON, HAILED REVOLUTIONARY FRANCE.

THE COMMERCIAL CLASSES, WITH HAMILTON, PREFERRED ENGLAND, THEIR MAIN SOURCE OF BUSINESS.

LIBERTY! EQUALITY! FRATERNITY!

MONEY! PROPERTY! STABILITY!

GRADUALLY, THE COUNTRY DIVIDED INTO TWO CAMPS...

THEY CALL THEM "PARTIES"?

EVEN THO THERE'S NOT A WOMAN IN EITHER OF 'EM!

BOTH PARTIES FAVORED THEIR OWN ELECTION AND THE OTHER'S REMOVAL!

HAMILTON'S PARTY, THE

FEDERALISTS,

FAVORED A STRONG CENTRAL GOVERNMENT, THE INTERESTS OF NORTHERN BANKERS AND MANUFACTURERS, ENGLAND OVER FRANCE, AND GOVERNMENT BY THE "BETTER SORT" (READ: BANKERS AND MANUFACTURERS).

ONE FEDERALIST PROPOSED A VOTING AGE OF 50!

JEFFERSON'S PARTY, THE

REPUBLICANS,

FAVORED A MINIMAL GOVERNMENT, THE INTERESTS OF FARMERS AND BORROWERS, THE SOUTH, FRANCE OVER ENGLAND, AND WIDER POPULAR PARTICIPATION IN GOVERNMENT.

GUILLOTINISTS!

AFTER TRYING TO STAY ABOVE THE FRAY, WASHINGTON FINALLY DECLARED HIMSELF A FEDERALIST. THE REPUBLICANS BEGAN CALLING HIM "TRAITOR," "VILLAIN," AND "ENEMY OF THE REVOLUTION," INSTEAD OF "MR. PRESIDENT."

IN 1796, WASHINGTON STARTED AN AMERICAN TRADITION BY ANNOUNCING THAT EIGHT YEARS AS PRESIDENT WAS MORE THAN ENOUGH FOR ANYONE. HE DECLINED TO RUN FOR A THIRD TERM, GIVING A FAREWELL ADDRESS BUT NO FORWARDING ADDRESS.

HE RETIRED TO HIS PLANTATION AND SUCCUMBED TO AN EXCESS OF MEDICAL TREATMENT.

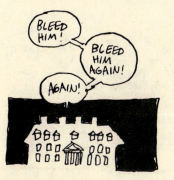

IN WASHINGTON'S LAST WILL & TESTAMENT, HE FREED ALL HIS SLAVES.

IN THE PRESIDENTIAL ELECTION OF 1796, THE FEDERALIST JOHN **ADAMS** WON NARROWLY OVER THE REPUBLICAN CANDIDATE, THOMAS JEFFERSON.

ASIDE FROM HIS DIAMETER, ADAMS IS BEST KNOWN FOR BUILDING UP THE NAVY WITH "OLD IRONSIDES" AND JAILING REPUBLICAN NEWSPAPER EDITORS WITH SEDITION LAWS.

SO WHY DID I LOSE IN 1800?

ADAMS' DEFEAT IN THE NEXT ELECTION SHOWS HOW IMPORTANT POLITICAL PARTIES HAD BECOME BY 1800.

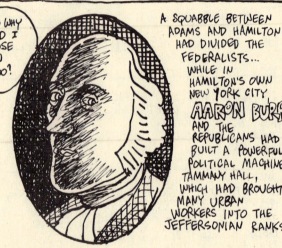

A SQUABBLE BETWEEN ADAMS AND HAMILTON HAD DIVIDED THE FEDERALISTS... WHILE IN HAMILTON'S OWN NEW YORK CITY **AARON BURR** AND THE REPUBLICANS HAD BUILT A POWERFUL POLITICAL MACHINE, TAMMANY HALL, WHICH HAD BROUGHT MANY URBAN WORKERS INTO THE JEFFERSONIAN RANKS.

BURR DELIVERED THE VOTES —

MANY OF THEM PERSONALLY!

NEW YORK WENT REPUBLICAN, SWINGING THE ELECTION TO JEFFERSON.

THEN BURR, WHO WAS THE VICE-PRESIDENTIAL CANDIDATE, TRIED TO STEAL THE PRESIDENCY FROM HIS RUNNING MATE! LATER, HE RUINED HIS POLITICAL LIFE TOTALLY BY KILLING ALEXANDER HAMILTON IN A DUEL...

MY CAREER IS SHOT!

THINK HOW I FEEL...

SO THOMAS JEFFERSON BECAME PRESIDENT...

SO WHAT?

TO UNDERSTAND WHAT THIS MEANT, YOU HAVE TO REALIZE HOW THE FEDERALISTS LOATHED THE MAN.

FOR YEARS, THE FEDERALISTS HAD BEEN TRYING TO HOLD BACK THE DEMOCRATIC TIDE. JEFFERSON THEY VIEWED AS A RADICAL... AN ATHEIST... A FRIEND OF THE FRENCH REVOLUTION, WHICH HAD MADE POLITICS SYNONYMOUS WITH DECAPITATION... A DREAMER WHOSE POLICIES WERE BASED ON THE HALLUCINATION OF EQUALITY. THE "FIRE-BREATHING SALAMANDER," THEY CALLED HIM.—AND NOW HE WAS PRESIDENT!!

WE'VE ELECTED AN AMPHIBIAN!

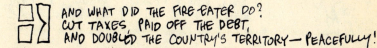

AND WHAT DID THE FIRE-EATER DO? CUT TAXES, PAID OFF THE DEBT, AND DOUBLED THE COUNTRY'S TERRITORY—PEACEFULLY!

117

FOR STARTERS, HE PEACEFULLY
DOUBLED THE NATION'S TERRITORY
WITH THE

LOUISIANA PURCHASE.

THE STORY
ACTUALLY
BEGINS WITH
ANOTHER
REVOLUTION,
THIS ONE
IN **HAITI**,
WHERE THE
SLAVES THREW
OFF, OR CUT
OFF, THEIR
FRENCH
MASTERS.

THE FRENCH
SET US SUCH
A GOOD
EXAMPLE!

(IN THE U.S.A., SOUTHERNERS
CRINGED IN FEAR, AND TRIED
TO KEEP THE NEWS FROM
THEIR OWN SLAVES.)

MIGHTY
QUIET...
MUST BE AN
UPRISING
SOMEWHERE...

ANYWAY, FRANCE THREW
HEAPS OF MEN, FRANCS,
AND BEANS INTO HAITI.
THE HAITIANS MADE
HAMBURGER OUT OF
THEM...

WHAT A
BARBECUE!

HM... NOW
MY WALLET'S
EMPTY...

NAPOLEON, WHO WAS NOW DICTATOR
OF FRANCE, DECIDED TO CASH IN HIS
AMERICAN REAL ESTATE. (HE EXPECTED
TO MAKE IT UP BY CONQUERING
RUSSIA, WHICH HAD LOTS OF OCEANFRONT,
OR AT LEAST PLENTY OF SERFS.)

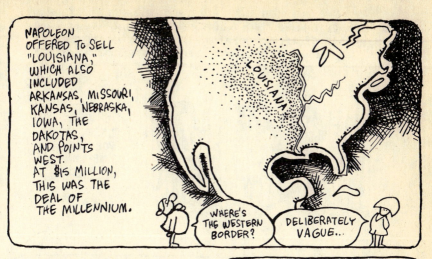

NAPOLEON OFFERED TO SELL "LOUISIANA," WHICH ALSO INCLUDED ARKANSAS, MISSOURI, KANSAS, NEBRASKA, IOWA, THE DAKOTAS, AND POINTS WEST. AT $15 MILLION, THIS WAS THE DEAL OF THE MILLENNIUM.

WHERE'S THE WESTERN BORDER?

DELIBERATELY VAGUE...

THE PRESIDENT FRANTICALLY FLIPPED THROUGH THE CONSTITUTION, LOOKING FOR A REAL ESTATE LICENSE...

C'MON! C'MON!

BONK BONK

NOT FINDING ONE, HE DID WHAT PRESIDENTS HAVE ALWAYS DONE:

WHATEVER I CAN GET AWAY WITH!

AND SO JEFFERSON CLOSED THE DEAL... AS FEDERALIST POLITICIANS MOANED HOW UNFAIR IT WAS OF HIM TO DO ANYTHING SO... SO... POPULAR...

"POPULAR!" THE VERY WORD LODGES IN MY ESOPHAGUS!

WE'LL SHOW 'EM... WE'LL DO SOMETHING POPULAR, TOO...

YEAH— LIKE LOSE THE NEXT ELECTION...

THE PRESIDENT IMMEDIATELY SHIPPED OFF TWO VIRGINIA NEIGHBORS, **LEWIS** AND **CLARK,** TO EXPLORE LOUISIANA — ALL THE WAY TO THE PACIFIC NORTHWEST, WHERE JEFFERSON HOPED TO PUT AN AMERICAN PORT.

HIS INDIAN POLICY WAS THEORETICALLY PEACEFUL, TOO... THAT IS, HE HOPED THAT THE INDIANS' CONTACTS WITH CIVILIZATION WOULD PERSUADE THEM TO ADOPT IT.

AND, IN DISPUTES WITH ENGLAND, FRANCE, AND SPAIN, JEFFERSON USED ONLY _ECONOMIC_ WARFARE— BOYCOTTS AND EMBARGOES— INSTEAD OF THE SHOOTING VARIETY. THIS PINCHED AMERICANS, TOO, BUT BETTER PINCHED THAN SHOT, YES?

AND DON'T FORGET THAT JEFFERSON REDUCED TAXES, CUT THE MILITARY BUDGET, AND PAID OFF THE NATIONAL DEBT!

NATURALLY, HE WAS RE-ELECTED BY A LANDSLIDE IN 1804.*

AT THIS, THE FEDERALISTS LOST THEIR HEADS — OR RATHER, THE FEDERALIST HEADS LOST CONTROL OF THEIR BODIES.

JOHN ADAMS, THE SECOND FEDERALIST PRESIDENT, TURNED OUT TO BE THE **LAST** FEDERALIST PRESIDENT.

BUT JEFFERSON'S PARTY IS STILL AROUND... WE KNOW IT AS THE **DEMOCRATIC** PARTY. (IT CHANGED NAMES AS SOON AS IT WAS SAFE.)

HE DIDN'T GUILLOTINE US — HE JUST DECAPITATED OUR PARTY!

*DURING THE CAMPAIGN, THE PRESS SPREAD DARK RUMORS (AND LIGHT VERSE) ABOUT JEFFERSON'S ALLEGED MEDIUM-DARK MISTRESS. HER NAME WAS SALLY HEMINGS, IT WAS SAID... SHE WAS HIS SLAVE... SHE BORE HIM FOUR CHILDREN, WHO ALL LOOKED AMAZINGLY LIKE THEIR DAD... ALL REMAINED IN SLAVERY... ETC... JEFFERSON, LIKE ANY SHARP POLITICIAN CONFRONTED WITH THE TRUTH, MADE NO COMMENT, AND LOST NO VOTES, APPARENTLY!

YOU'D VOTE FOR ME, IF YOU COULD VOTE, WOULDN'T YOU, SAL?

NO COMMENT.

JEFFERSON'S LEGACY

IMPRESSIVE AS HIS ACCOMPLISHMENTS
WERE, JEFFERSON'S CONTRADICTIONS
WERE EQUALLY AMAZING! WHAT CAN
YOU SAY ABOUT A MAN WHO—

BELIEVED THAT STATE &
LOCAL GOVERNMENT WERE
CLOSEST TO THE PEOPLE...

...WHEN HIS OWN STATE
WAS DOMINATED BY A
SLAVEOWNING ELITE?

SAW AMERICA'S FUTURE
AS A NATION OF
YEOMAN FARMERS...

...AT THE DAWN OF
THE INDUSTRIAL AGE?

OPPOSED SLAVERY IN
PUBLIC...

...ENJOYED SLAVERY
IN PRIVATE?

BELIEVED THAT BLACKS
WERE OPPRESSED...

...BELIEVED THAT
BLACKS WERE INFERIOR?

THOUGHT URBAN
WORKERS WERE
IRRESPONSIBLE CITIZENS...

...WELCOMED URBAN
WORKERS INTO HIS
PARTY?

ADVOCATED THE SIMPLE
LIFE...

...LIVED A LIFE OF
LUXURY?

EXPRESSED SYMPATHY
FOR THE INDIANS...

...FOUNDED THE
DETESTED INDIAN
BUREAU?

BELIEVED IN A
FREE PRESS...

...SECRETLY
SUBSIDIZED A NEWS-
PAPER TO FLAY
HIS ENEMIES?

DEMANDED A STRICT
INTERPRETATION OF
THE CONSTITUTION...

...STRETCHED THE
CONSTITUTION TO
BUY LOUISIANA?

OO...
I FEEL
A
MIGRAINE
COMING
ON...

WHAT, INDEED, CAN YOU SAY ?

YOU
CAN SAY
HE'S A
LIBERAL...

WELL, YOU CAN SAY THAT HE FOUNDED AN ENDURING
POLITICAL PARTY IN HIS OWN IMAGE — FULL
OF CONTRADICTIONS, THAT IS: THE PARTY
OF THE WHITE RACIST AND THE BLACKS,
THE ETHNIC AND THE BIGOT, THE
FACTORY WORKER AND THE YUPPIE,
THE SOCIALIST AND THE
CONSERVATIVE, THE SOUTHERNER
FOR STATES' RIGHTS AND THE
NORTHERNER FOR BIG
GOVERNMENT, THE
EXPANSIONIST, THE
CONTRACTIONIST...

AND OCCASIONALLY,
THE CONTORTIONIST!

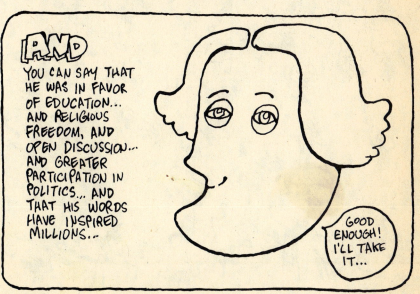

AND

YOU CAN SAY THAT
HE WAS IN FAVOR
OF EDUCATION...
AND RELIGIOUS
FREEDOM, AND
OPEN DISCUSSION...
AND GREATER
PARTICIPATION IN
POLITICS... AND
THAT HIS WORDS
HAVE INSPIRED
MILLIONS...

GOOD
ENOUGH!
I'LL TAKE
IT...

123

12A

CHAPTER 8

MANIFEST DENTISTRY, OR THE GREAT UPROOTING

WITH VISIONS OF JEFFERSONIAN RHETORIC DANCING IN THEIR HEADS, AMERICANS FLOODED WEST IN THE EARLY 1800's... THE ACTION WAS IN OHIO, INDIANA, AND ILLINOIS IN THE NORTH, AND GEORGIA, MISSISSIPPI, AND ALABAMA, DOWN SOUTH.

BY GOLLY, MAW, LET'S CARVE US A FARM FROM TH' VIRGIN FOREST INHABITED ONLY BY WILD BEASTS & NEKKID SAVAGES WHO WILL QUICKLY SEE THE ADVANTAGES OF CIVILIZED LIFE!

UNFORTUNATELY, IT DIDN'T QUITE WORK OUT ACCORDING TO THE PEACEABLE JEFFERSONIAN PLAN... FOR SOME REASON, THE VANGUARD OF CIVILIZATION DIDN'T EXACTLY INSPIRE THE INDIANS TO IMITATION...

LAND SPECULATORS...

I'LL GIVE YOU A MOUNTAIN OF TRINKETS FOR A MOUNTAIN!

WHISKEY PEDDLERS (OFTEN INDISTINGUISHABLE FROM LAND SPECULATORS)...

I'LL THROW THIS IN FOR FREE!

AND WORST OF ALL, OUTRIGHT INDIAN-KILLERS WHO COULD NEVER BE BROUGHT TO JUSTICE IN ANY U.S. COURT.

GOOD SHOT, LEM! KILL HER AGAIN!

126

INDIAN RESISTANCE WAS LED BY TWO SHAWNEE BROTHERS, **TENSKWATAWA**, "THE PROPHET," AND **TECUMSEH**, THE WARRIOR. TECUMSEH IS THE MORE FAMOUS OF THE TWO, AS HIS NAME IS EASIER TO PRONOUNCE.

"THE PROPHET"

TECUMSEH

THE PROPHET, WHO PREACHED THE REJECTION OF ALL THINGS PERTAINING TO THE U.S.A., WON MANY CONVERTS BY PREDICTING A SOLAR ECLIPSE, WHICH HE HAD HEARD ABOUT FROM SOME AMERICAN ASTRONOMERS IN 1806.

TECUMSEH, WHO RELIED MORE ON LOGIC, TRAVELED FROM CANADA TO ALABAMA, TRYING TO ORGANIZE A MILITARY ALLIANCE OF ALL THE TRIBES.

BY 1811, FEDERAL TROOPS WERE MARCHING ON THE PROPHET'S HEADQUARTERS. THE RESULT WAS THE BATTLE OF **TIPPECANOE** (INDIANA), AND THE CONCLUSION WAS INESCAPABLE: THIS WAS WAR!

THANK GOD JEFFERSON'S NOT STILL PRESIDENT!

AND SO THE U.S.
DID THE ONLY LOGICAL
THING: DECLARED
WAR — ON
GREAT BRITAIN!!

THIS
WAS
THE

WAR OF 1812

(WHICH WAS PROMOTED BY WESTERN "WAR HAWKS" WHO
COVETED CANADA AND HOPED TO STOP BRITISH SUPPLIES FROM
REACHING TECUMSEH).

NOT TO MENTION
AN EXCELLENT
EXCUSE TO GRAB
SOME MORE
INDIAN LAND!!

AMONG
OTHER
REASONS...

HENRY
CLAY..

WARK!
WARK!

THE U.S. FOUGHT BRITAIN
TO A STANDSTILL...
MOST OF THE STANDING STILL
TOOK PLACE ALONG THE
CANADIAN BORDER. THERE WAS
ALSO SOME RUNNING, WHEN THE
REDCOATS BURNED WASHINGTON, D.C.,
AND THE OCCASIONAL SINKING
SENSATION, ESPECIALLY AFTER
NAVAL BATTLES...

PASS THE
DRAMAMINE...

128

BUT FOR THE INDIANS, THE WAR OF 1812 WAS A DISASTER...
TECUMSEH FELL IN LATE 1813, NEAR THE CANADIAN BORDER.

(HE IS USUALLY CONSIDERED THE GREATEST OF MODERN INDIAN STATESMEN + WARRIORS...)

EVEN WORSE WAS THE ARRIVAL OF **ANDREW JACKSON,** WHOSE NICKNAME WAS "OLD HICKORY," BUT COULD HAVE BEEN "THE TERMINATOR." AS A BOY, JACKSON HAD LOST HIS FAMILY IN THE REVOLUTION... THIS MADE HIM A FAIRLY TESTY FELLOW... HE WAS ALWAYS CHALLENGING PEOPLE TO DUELS... AND AT TIMES IT SEEMED THAT HE TOOK GENUINE PLEASURE IN KILLING PEOPLE!!

IN 1813, JACKSON LED A CAMPAIGN AGAINST THE CREEK INDIANS IN THE SOUTH... YOU COULD FOLLOW HIS TRAIL BY THE BODIES OF SOLDIERS HANGED FOR DESERTION, INSUBORDINATION, COMPLAINING ABOUT THE FOOD, ETC...

JACKSON INVITED, OR
TERRORIZED, HUNDREDS
OF CREEKS AND
CHEROKEES INTO HIS ARMY...
AND THEN SENT THEM TO
LEAD THE CHARGE AGAINST
THEIR COUSINS...

THEN HE "REWARDED" HIS ALLIES WITH A TREATY
THAT TOOK AS MUCH LAND FROM THEM AS FROM
THEIR ENEMIES! (THIS WAS PART OF GEORGIA AND
MOST OF ALABAMA...)

NEXT HE MARCHED HIS ARMY TO NEW ORLEANS AND DEFEATED THE BRITISH IN A HUGE BATTLE WHICH MADE JACKSON A **NATIONAL HERO**... IRONICALLY, THE PEACE TREATY HAD ALREADY BEEN SIGNED, BUT WORD HADN'T ARRIVED FROM EUROPE YET...

IF THE TELEGRAPH EXISTED, I'D JUST BE ANOTHER SEMI-HOMICIDAL MANIAC FROM TENNESSEE!

AND, FOR HIS FINAL EXPLOIT OF THE 18-TEENS, JACKSON MADE A SEMI-UNAUTHORIZED INVASION OF SPANISH **FLORIDA**. THERE HE KILLED INDIANS, DESTROYED A FORTFUL OF ESCAPED SLAVES, HANGED A COUPLE ENGLISHMEN... AND CONVINCED SPAIN TO SELL FLORIDA CHEAP... WASHINGTON TOOK NOTE!

HIS METHODS ARE CRUDE, VICIOUS, ILLEGAL, AND UNCONSTITUTIONAL, BUT HIS **BODY COUNT** IS ASTONISHING!

A FUTURE IN POLITICS LOOMS...

ALL OURS!

WITHIN TEN YEARS, JACKSON WAS PRESIDENT— THE FIRST WESTERNER IN THE OFFICE...

UNTIL 1828, EVERY PRESIDENT EITHER CAME FROM VIRGINIA, OR WAS NAMED ADAMS!

JACKSON PROCEEDED TO "OPEN" THE WEST—

AS IN, "OPEN WIDE!"

(NOTE: JACKSON HIMSELF WAS A BIG SPECULATOR IN WESTERN REAL ESTATE.)

THE FEDERAL GOVERNMENT, WHICH HAD GUARANTEED CERTAIN LANDS TO THE INDIANS, NOW LOOKED THE OTHER WAY AS THEY WERE TAKEN AWAY BY WHITE SETTLERS, STATE LAWS, AND PLAIN, OLD FRAUD...

AND WHEN WE RESIST, THEY CALL IT "RAVAGING THE FRONTIER SETTLEMENTS!"

FINALLY, WHEN FIGHTING BROKE OUT AGAIN, THE PRES UNVEILED HIS REAL PLANS, WHICH TOOK THE NAME OF

REMOVAL.

AT LEAST IT'S AN HONEST NAME!

THE IDEA WAS DAZZLINGLY SIMPLE: JUST "REMOVE" ALL THE INDIANS ON THE EAST SIDE OF THE MISSISSIPPI RIVER ACROSS TO THE WEST SIDE, TO "INDIAN TERRITORY" (OKLAHOMA). SIMPLICITY ITSELF!!

CONGRESS VOTED, AND IT WAS DONE... TRIBE AFTER TRIBE WAS MARCHED OFF BY THE CAVALRY... CHICKASAWS, CHOCTAWS, CREEKS, CHEROKEES, SHAWNEES, SACS, FOXES... 70,000 IN ALL... AND ALL BADLY SUPPLIED WITH FOOD AND BLANKETS, SO THAT THOUSANDS DIED ALONG THE WAY... 4500 CHEROKEES ALONE...

MARTIN VAN BUREN, THE NEXT PRESIDENT, CALLED IT "A HAPPY AND CERTAIN CONSUMMATION" OF A "WISE, HUMANE, AND UNDEVIATING POLICY," WHILE CHEROKEES STILL CALL IT THE TRAIL OF TEARS.

SO—IF YOU EVER HEAR THE QUESTION ASKED, "CAN 'IT' HAPPEN HERE?"— THE ANSWER IS:

BEFORE TAKING LEAVE OF ANDREW JACKSON, WE SHOULD NOTE THAT HE WAS ONE OF ONLY TWO PRESIDENTS WHOSE NAMES BECAME ADJECTIVES, AS IN ⟹

(THE OTHER ONE WAS JEFFERSON.)

WHAT WAS DEMOCRACY, JACKSON-STYLE? ACTUALLY, IT'S EASIER TO SAY WHAT "JEFFERSONIAN" MEANT, BECAUSE JEFFERSON, A THINKER AND WRITER, HAD A THEORY OF SOCIETY. IN JEFFERSON'S VIEW, DEMOCRACY SHOULD BE BASED ON A SELF-SUFFICIENT MIDDLE CLASS OF "YEOMAN FARMERS," WHOSE IDEAS WOULD BE FORMED BY LIBERAL EDUCATION AND A FREE PRESS. GOVERNMENT SHOULD BE MINIMAL AND TAXES LOW.

THANKS, TOM!

"JACKSONIAN" DEMOCRACY, ON THE OTHER HAND, WAS NOT THE PRODUCT OF ANY ONE MIND. IT SIMPLY MEANT WHATEVER DEMOCRACY HAD BECOME BY THE TIME ANDREW JACKSON HAPPENED ALONG. (IRONICALLY, THE CONSERVATIVE JACKSON HAD ALMOST NOTHING TO DO WITH ITS DEVELOPMENT.)

I DIDN'T EVEN LIKE IT, UNTIL IT ELECTED ME PRESIDENT!

ITS ELEMENTS:

UNIVERSAL MANHOOD SUFFRAGE: BEGINNING IN THE WEST, STATES HAD BEGUN EXTENDING THE VOTE TO ALL (WHITE) MEN, REGARDLESS OF PROPERTY. THIS WAS THE DEMOCRACY OF ALL SOCIAL CLASSES.

THERE ARE GREASY STAINS ON THE WHITE HOUSE WALLS!

RAPID EXPANSION OF THE WEST: JACKSONIANS ASSAILED "EASTERN MONEY," WHOSE CONSERVATISM SLOWED WESTERN GROWTH... THEY FAVORED EASY MONEY + PLENTY OF SPECULATION, EVEN IF THESE PRODUCED A CHAOTIC, BOOM/BUST ECONOMY WITH FREQUENT BANK FAILURES.

10TH NAT'L BANK OF 11TH STREET

CLOSED

TIME TO GO WEST AGAIN!

(AND OF COURSE INDIAN REMOVAL WAS A BIG PART OF WESTERN EXPANSION.)

THE PRESIDENT AS REPRESENTATIVE OF ALL THE PEOPLE: PREVIOUSLY, CONGRESS HAD BEEN CONSIDERED THE MOST "POPULAR" BRANCH... BUT JACKSON FREELY VETOED CONGRESSIONAL BILLS AND FEUDED OPENLY WITH THE SUPREME COURT. JACKSON SET THE MODEL FOR THE BORN-ON-THE-FRONTIER, NOT-ESPECIALLY WELL-EDUCATED, MILITARY-HERO TYPE PRESIDENT.

VETO

"KING ANDREW", HIS ENEMIES CALLED HIM...

135

MEANWHILE

(ON ANOTHER FRONT...)

THE BROOM
OF REVOLUTION
WAS SWEEPING
SPAIN OUT OF
LATIN AMERICA...
BY 1823, ONLY
THE MOPPING
UP WAS
LEFT...

SO THE UNITED STATES, IN THE PERSON OF PRESIDENT **MONROE**, ISSUED A **DOCTRINE**. (THIS WAS CHEAPER THAN SENDING AID TO THE REVOLUTIONARIES.) FROM NOW ON, SAID THE DOCTRINE, THE U.S. WOULD NO LONGER TOLERATE EUROPEANS WHO PILLAGED THE AMERICAS... FOR SOME REASON, THE NEWLY INDEPENDENT NATIONS TOOK THIS TO MEAN THAT ALL FUTURE PILLAGING WOULD BE DONE BY THE U.S.A. ALONE...

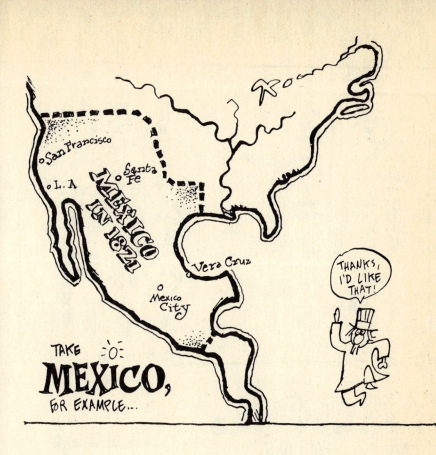

TAKE
MEXICO,
FOR EXAMPLE...

MEXICAN
INDEPENDENCE
CAME IN 1821...
AS YOU CAN SEE,
IT WAS A BIG
PLACE THEN...
MUST HAVE
BEEN NICE, TOO...
BECAUSE
AMERICANS
KEPT MOVING
THERE...

I WONDER WHAT'S SO BAD AT HOME THAT MAKES THEM LEAVE??

137

A FEW PARTS OF MEXICO
THE GRINGOS INVADED:

TEXAS

ANGLOS (AND SLAVES) BEGAN
SETTLING IN THE 1820'S...
THEY RAISED BIG CATTLE WITH
LONG HORNS ON HUGE RANCHES...
EVERYTHING ABOUT THE PLACE
WAS BIG... THE QUANTITY OF BULL
WAS ENORMOUS... ESPECIALLY
WHEN THE TEXANS SWORE LOYALTY
TO MEXICO... WAR BROKE OUT
IN 1836 – REMEMBER THE ALAMO?
TEXAS BECAME A REPUBLIC...
THEN A STATE OF THE UNION
AND A STATE OF MIND...

CALIFORNIA

CALIFORNIA WAS FAR AWAY,
BUT FAR OUT... THE
PRINCIPAL INDUSTRY
WAS GOING ON HIKES...
NEVERTHELESS, WHEN
CAPT. **JOHN FRÉMONT'S**
TROOPS SWOOPED OVER
THE SIERRA, A DOZEN
MEN BESTIRRED
THEMSELVES TO
PROCLAIM THE
*BEAR FLAG
REPUBLIC* IN 1846.

138

UTAH

IN 1847, SALT LAKE CITY WAS FOUNDED BY THE MORMONS, WHO WERE FLEEING RELIGIOUS PERSECUTION, A GRAND AMERICAN TRADITION.* THE ONLY DIFFERENCE WAS, THIS PERSECUTION WAS IN THE UNITED STATES. UTAH SEEMED SAFE, AS WHO ELSE WOULD WANT IT?

BRIGAAM YOUNG AND FOLLOWERS

THE MORMONS GOT ALONG FINE WITH THE MEXICANS AND INDIANS... IT WAS THE AMERICANS THEY DETESTED... IN FACT, ONE OF **THE MOUNTAIN MEADOWS MASSACRES**, IN WHICH MORMONS AND PAIUTES COMBINED TO SLAUGHTER OVER 100 MEN, WOMEN, & KIDS ON THEIR WAY TO CALIFORNIA...

OKAY, GUYS! GIT 'EM!

OREGON

JUST TO PROVE THAT THEY WEREN'T PICKING ON MEXICO, AMERICANS ALSO FLOODED OREGON, WHICH WAS CLAIMED BY BRITAIN, AND WAS USUALLY FLOODED ALREADY.

IT HASN'T LET UP SINCE LEWIS & CLARK...

*FLEEING, THAT IS, NOT PERSECUTION

139

SUDDENLY, THE AMERICAN PUBLIC AND PRESS DISCOVERED THAT THEIR COUNTRY HAD A "MANIFEST DESTINY" TO SPREAD FROM SEA TO SEA... THIS HAD NEVER BEEN PARTICULARLY MANIFEST BEFORE, ESPECIALLY TO MEXICANS...

FUNNY, IT DOESN'T **LOOK** LIKE THE UNITED STATES...

POLKING IT INTO HIM.

PRESIDENT POLK, A PROTÉGÉ OF ANDREW JACKSON, KNEW HOW TO START A FIGHT: IN 1846 HE SENT TROOPS INTO MEXICO... WHEN THE MEXICAN ARMY SHOT AT THEM, POLK SQUEALED THAT "OUR BOYS" NEEDED PROTECTION!!

CONGRESS BICKERED CONFUSEDLY... SOME SAID POLK WAS A SNEAKY, SLIMY, BALD-FACED LIAR... OTHERS SAID OF COURSE HE IS, BUT HE'S ALSO THE PRESIDENT AND COMMANDER-IN-CHIEF... WITH THAT REASSURING THOUGHT, CONGRESS VOTED MONEY FOR FIGHTING, BUT WITHHELD A DECLARATION OF WAR...

A FINE COMPROMISE!

140

AND SO BEGAN

THE MEXICAN WAR —

FIRST OF A LINE OF UNDECLARED WARS...
THE MARINES LANDED
IN MEXICO, AND THE
INVASION HEADED FOR
THE "HALLS OF
MONTEZUMA."

HERE'S TO
THE MONROE
DOCTRINE!

THE NAVY SAILED FOR THE COAST, WHILE THE CAVALRY VISITED
SUNNY NEW MEXICO...

IS DIS
DA WAY
TO
HOLLYWOOD?

WHEN IT WAS OVER
IN 1848, MEXICO WAS
MINUS HALF ITS
LAND, AND THE U.S.A.
HAD SWOLLEN TO
ITS FAMILIAR
SHAPE. (OREGON
HAD BEEN ACQUIRED
PEACEFULLY.)

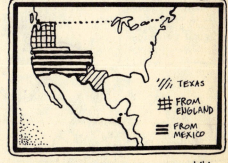

/// TEXAS

FROM
ENGLAND

≡ FROM
MEXICO

POSTSCRIPT TO CHAPTER 8:
THE GOLD RUSH

IN 1848, JUST AFTER CALIFORNIA WAS ACQUIRED, THE STUFF THAT DRIVES MEN MAD WAS FOUND THERE...

ACID? SPEED? OH— GOLD!

THEY CAME FROM CHILE, CHINA, CHICAGO...

DUST NUGGETS INGOTS LITTLE CHAINS...

SAN FRANCISCO EXPLODED INTO AN INSTANT CITY OF MUD, TENTS, SHACKS, HARD MEN AND EASY WOMEN, EASY MONEY AND HARD LUCK... A HARBOR OF ROTTING, ABANDONED SHIPS... PANTS CUT FROM SAILCLOTH BY LEVI STRAUSS...

EE-HAW!

WHENEVER THINGS GOT TOO FAR OUT OF HAND, THE GOOD CITIZENS WOULD STRING UP A MURDERER. THIS ENCOURAGED OTHER MURDERERS TO LEAVE TOWN...

THEY FILLED ARIZONA WITH THE "MOST VILLAINOUS COLLECTION OF WHITE MEN THAT EVER BREATHED" (IN ONE HISTORIAN'S LOVELY PHRASE).

IN JUST TWO YEARS, CALIFORNIA WAS ASKING FOR STATEHOOD, AND PLUNGING THE UNION INTO CRISIS... BUT YOU'LL HAVE TO GET THROUGH THE NEXT CHAPTER BEFORE YOU LEARN WHAT THAT WAS ABOUT...

CHAPTER 9
RAILROADS, OVER- AND UNDERGROUND

Yes, the young country was on the move, and not only westward... It was also blasting full steam ahead into the Industrial Revolution...

IT ALL
STARTED
WITH THE
COTTON GIN,
WHICH WAS
A MACHINE,
NOT A
BEVERAGE...

THE GIN
SPEEDED UP
COTTONSEED
PULLING
5000%
AND BOOSTED
PROFITS
ENORMOUSLY.

SUDDENLY, IN THE SOUTH,
COTTON FIELDS ROLLED
WESTWARD AS FAST
AS ANDY JACKSON
COULD CLEAR THE WAY...

SNAP
CRUNCH
EEYAH!
EEYAH! ⭑ ⭑ BANG
BANG BANG

144

THE NORTH ALSO DERIVED BENEFITS FROM THE "COTTON KINGDOM"-- FEDERAL TAXES ON THE SOUTH SUBSIDIZED NORTHERN EXPANSION...

THE NORTH SPROUTED HIGHWAYS, BRIDGES, CANALS, RAILROADS, AND FACTORIES THAT BELCHED SOOT WITHOUT SAYING, "EXCUSE ME!"

I'M BAD! I'M RUDE!

(THE NORTH ALSO SPROUTED NEW FORESTS, AS FARMERS ABANDONED THEIR FARMS TO SEEK WORK IN THE FACTORY TOWNS...)

145

Industrialization changed more than the landscape...

IT CHANGED PEOPLE'S LIVES...

LITTLE THINGS LIKE: SENDING LARGE NUMBERS OF WOMEN INTO THE FACTORIES... MAKING THEM STAND AT A MACHINE 15 HOURS A DAY... NEVER LETTING THEM SEE THE SUN... THINGS LIKE THAT...

MEANWHILE, TRANSATLANTIC STEAMSHIPS BROUGHT MILLIONS OF IMMIGRANTS TO FEED THE NEW FACTORIES.

THE IMMIGRANTS, MOSTLY IRISH AND GERMANS, FLED THE FAMINES AND FAILED REVOLUTIONS OF EUROPE.

THEY CROWDED INTO AMERICA'S CITIES, WHERE THEY FOUND OPPORTUNITY — AS WELL AS SLUMS, PERSISTENT PREJUDICE,* JOB DISCRIMINATION, AND OCCASIONAL RIOTS.

HELP WANTED NO IRISH NEED APPLY

WE'LL SHOW 'EM! WE'LL TAKE OVER CITY HALL!

⟹ *NO IRISH CATHOLIC WAS ELECTED PRESIDENT UNTIL JOHN F. KENNEDY IN 1960!

147

IT WAS ALSO THE

Age of Reform

(THERE WAS SO MUCH TO REFORM!)

FREEDOM OF ASSOCIATION WAS
GUARANTEED BY THE CONSTITUTION,
SO AMERICANS GOT TOGETHER
AND FREE-ASSOCIATED... THIS
WAS SUPPOSED TO CURE SOCIETY'S
ILLS...

AT LEAST IT FEELS
SAFER STANDING CLOSE
TOGETHER LIKE THIS...

THEY ASSOCIATED IN:

* LABOR UNIONS,
TO IMPROVE
WORKING CONDITIONS

* RELIGIONS, NEW
AND USED

* SOCIETIES TO
PROMOTE EDUCATION

* UTOPIAN
COMMUNITIES, TO
ACHIEVE PERFECTION

* ANTI-SLAVERY
SOCIETIES

* PLAIN OLD POLITICAL
PARTIES

* FACTIONS WITHIN
POLITICAL PARTIES

* ASSORTED GROUPS
OF PACIFISTS,
PRISON REFORMERS,
TEMPERANCE
ADVOCATES,
ETC...

AND
THE
WOMEN'S
MOVEMENT?

NOT
YET...
NOT YET...

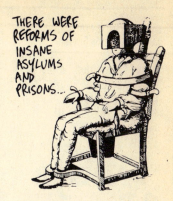

THERE WERE REFORMS OF INSANE ASYLUMS AND PRISONS...

MANY OF THESE REFORMERS HAD CAUSE FOR CELEBRATION IN THE 1820's, '30's, AND '40's. FOR EXAMPLE, THE VOTE WAS FINALLY GIVEN TO ALL WHITE MEN, REGARDLESS OF PROPERTY..

FREE PUBLIC SCHOOLS BEGAN TO OPEN HERE AND THERE...

NOW THAT I'VE GOT IT, I'M KEEPIN' IT TO MYSELF!

BALLOTS

彡#🕱👁@🕱 REFORMERS!!

THE LABOR MOVEMENT MADE MODEST GAINS... AT LEAST, UNIONS WERE LEGALIZED BY THE SUPREME COURT IN 1842...

THIS IS GONNA BE A LONG STRUGGLE..

SO TELL ME — HAVE YOU NOTICED ANYTHING MISSING FROM THE LIST?

STRANGELY ENOUGH,
ALL THESE CHANGES
HAPPENED UP NORTH...
DOWN SOUTH, THE ONLY
MOVEMENT WAS THE
PRICE OF SLAVES
GOING UP AND DOWN...

NO MORE
MR. NICE
GUY!!

ANTI-SLAVERY
ACTIVISTS, TIRED
OF SEEING EVERY
OTHER REFORM GROUP
MAKING PROGRESS,
EXCEPT THEMSELVES,
ANGRILY CHANGED
THEIR TUNE — FROM
FLAT TO SHARP...

$1200
TO
1250 DOLLARS!
— FOR NEGROES!!

THEIR NEW LEAD VOCALIST WAS

WILLIAM LLOYD
GARRISON,

AND HIS LYRICS WERE LIKE
A BREATH FROM A
BLAST FURNACE... SLAVEOWNERS
WERE "MAN-STEALERS,"
"WOMAN-FLOGGERS," "RAPISTS,"
"MURDERERS..." THE U.S.
CONSTITUTION, THANKS TO
ITS PRO-SLAVERY CLAUSES,
WAS A "PACT WITH HELL."

MOMMY!
THAT MAN
INSULTED THE
CONSTITUTION!

KILL
HIM!

150

GARRISON PUT ON QUITE A
SHOW — EVERY PERFORMANCE
WAS MOBBED... THESE WERE
NOT THE SORT OF MOBS THAT
TURN UGLY... THEY WERE
UGLY TO BEGIN WITH... AND ALL
BECAUSE GARRISON SAID THAT
THE FOUNDING FATHERS WERE
"HYPOCRITES" AND THAT THE
NATION SHOULD BE DISMEMBERED
("NO UNION WITH SLAVEHOLDERS!").

OF COURSE THESE MOBS WERE WHITE... TO BLACKS, GARRISON
MADE PERFECT SENSE. FOR YEARS, BLACK ABOLITIONISTS
HAD BEEN WAITING PATIENTLY FOR A WHITE MAN THIS
IMPATIENT, AND NOW HE WAS HERE. OVER HALF THE
SUBSCRIBERS TO GARRISON'S NEWSPAPER, THE LIBERATOR, WERE BLACK.

ANOTHER ABOLITIONIST NOVELTY, BESIDES THEIR RHETORIC, WAS THAT WOMEN SPOKE PUBLICLY AT THEIR MEETINGS. THIS WAS THOUGHT TO BE IMPOSSIBLE, UNTIL IT HAPPENED, AFTER WHICH IT BECAME MERELY IMPROPER, SUBVERSIVE, UNFEMININE, AND OUTSIDE "WOMAN'S PROPER SPHERE."

PIECES OF SPHERE

SARAH GRIMKÉ

ANGELINA GRIMKÉ

(WOMAN'S SPHERE, IN CASE YOU WONDERED, WAS COOKING, WASHING, BABIES, AND BEING SUPPORTIVE EVEN WHEN YOU'RE NOT BEING SUPPORTED.)

LET ME OUT OF HERE!

IN 1840, A WORLD ANTI-SLAVERY MEETING IN LONDON SPLIT OVER THE "WOMAN QUESTION." AFTER HEARING CIRCULAR ARGUMENTS IN FAVOR OF WOMAN'S SPHERE, THE MALE DELEGATES BANISHED THE FEMALES TO THE BALCONY.

I'VE HEARD OF PUTTING US ON A PEDESTAL, BUT A BALCONY?

AND SPEAKING OF WOMEN, LET'S NOT FORGET THE INCREDIBLE

HARRIET TUBMAN,

ALSO KNOWN AS "MOSES."

(A SMALL WOMAN WITH A LARGE PRICE ON HER HEAD)

SHE WAS THE CHIEF CONDUCTOR OF THE "UNDERGROUND RAILWAY," WHICH, UNLIKE THE REAL RAILWAY, DIDN'T RUN ON RAILS... THE PURPOSE OF THE UNDERGROUND RAILWAY WAS TO BRING SLAVES TO FREEDOM OR CANADA, WHICHEVER CAME FIRST.

FALSE BOTTOM →

OVERGROUND RAILWAY CARS

UNDERGROUND RAILWAY VEHICLES

MS TUBMAN, AN ESCAPED SLAVE HERSELF, MADE *NINETEEN* TRIPS INTO THE SOUTH TO RESCUE HER FELLOW SLAVES...

AND BELIEVE ME, I TOOK A GUN!!

AFTERWARDS, SEVERAL
ABOLITIONIST WOMEN,
TIRED OF GEOMETRY
LESSONS, DECIDED
THEY HAD BETTER
FIGHT FOR THEIR
OWN RIGHTS, TOO...

THE WOMEN'S MOVEMENT

WAS BORN IN
1848... THAT'S
WHEN
**LUCRETIA MOTT,
ELIZABETH CADY
STANTON, JANE
HUNT, MARTHA
WRIGHT,** AND
MARY ANN McCLINTOCK
CALLED THE FIRST
WOMAN'S RIGHTS
CONVENTION IN
SENECA FALLS, N.Y.
THIS MEETING WAS A
SUCCESS — THE ONLY
PROBLEM WAS LIMITING
THE AGENDA, THERE
WERE SO MANY
WRONGS TO
RIGHT...

IT TOOK MORE THAN SIXTY
YEARS TO WIN THE VOTE...
SO WE'LL SAVE THE STORY
FOR VOLUME 2... MEANWHILE,
CHECK OUT THE UNISEX
FEMINIST FASHIONS OF
THE 1850'S:

153

FORMER SLAVES TELLING
THE AWFUL TRUTH...
WHITE ABOLITIONISTS
FLINGING INSULTS...
A BLACK INTELLECTUAL
SUPERIOR TO ANY
WHITE IN THE SOUTH...
**BLACK WOMEN
WITH GUNS??**

HOW WERE THE
SLAVEOWNERS TO
RESPOND TO *THIS?*

IT'S ALL TH'
FAULT O' THET
ABOLISH-NEST
LIDDY-CHUR!

ONE NOT PARTICULARLY
IMAGINATIVE WAY WAS
WITH CENSORSHIP —
LIKE THE "GAG RULE"
FORBIDDING CONGRESSIONAL
DEBATE ON ABOLITIONIST
PETITIONS...

CONSTITUTION SEZ
TH' PEOPLE HAVE A
RIGHT TO PETITION,
NOT THAT TH'
GUMMINT GOTTA
LISTEN...

...OR BANNING
"INSURRECTIONARY"
(I.E., ANTI-SLAVERY)
MATERIAL FROM THE
U.S. MAILS IN
THE SOUTH...

WHUZZAT?
"ALL MEN ARE
CREATED EQUAL"?
"ENDOWED WITH
INALIENABLE
RIGHTS"?
GET OUTA HERE!

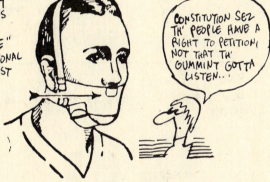

EQUALLY IMPRESSIVE WAS

FREDERICK DOUGLASS,

ANOTHER RUNAWAY... HE
TURNED UP AT AN ABOLITIONIST
MEETING IN 1841, AND
WITHIN A YEAR OR TWO
HE WAS THEIR GREATEST
SPEAKER — AND A
CANDIDATE FOR LARGEST
HAIR OF THE 1840's...

IN A COLOR-BLIND SOCIETY, DOUGLASS COULD HAVE BEEN
PRESIDENT. AS IT WAS, HE HAD TO SETTLE FOR BECOMING THE
"FIRST BLACK TO..."

⇨ RUN HIS OWN
NEWSPAPER

⇨ ADVISE PRESIDENTS

⇨ BE A U.S.
DIPLOMAT

⇨ MAKE A FORTUNE
ON THE LECTURE
CIRCUIT

AND TO THINK
THAT HE
LEARNED TO
READ BY
TRADING HIS
LUNCH TO
WHITE BOYS
FOR LESSONS!

"THERE IS NOT A MAN
BENEATH THE CANOPY OF
HEAVEN, THAT DOES NOT
KNOW THAT SLAVERY
IS WRONG FOR HIM,"
HE POINTED OUT.

155

THE ANSWER IS UNDOUBTEDLY, "ALL OF THE ABOVE..." BUT WHATEVER THE UNDERLYING ISSUES, THE IMMEDIATE IRRITANT WAS THIS QUESTION: SHOULD SLAVERY BE ALLOWED IN THE VAST TERRITORIES ACQUIRED* IN THE MEXICAN WAR??

WE STOLE IT — WHY NOT ENSLAVE IT?

BETWEEN 1800 AND 1850, THE NORTH HAD BOOMED DEAFENINGLY, WHILE THE SOUTH SOMEHOW SLEPT THROUGH IT... NOW THE SOUTH WANTED TO EXPLODE, TOO... THIS REQUIRED EXPANSION... BUT FOR SOME REASON, THE SLAVEOWNER COULDN'T CONCEIVE OF DOING BUSINESS WITHOUT BEING ABLE TO BUY AND SELL HIS WORKERS.

AH'M A FAHMUH, NOT A THINKUH...

*OR, DEPENDING ON YOUR MOOD OR OPINION: CONQUERED, WRESTED, CEDED, GRABBED, JUSTLY WON, EXTORTED, ETC...

CHAPTER 10

IN WHICH A WAR IS FOUGHT,
FOR SOME REASON...

EVERYONE HAS A THEORY OF WHY THE CIVIL WAR WAS FOUGHT...

THE SOUTH SAID IT WAS A QUESTION OF STATES' RIGHTS...

THE NORTH SAID IT WAS TO PRESERVE THE UNION...

SOME BLAMED THE SPREAD OF SLAVERY; OTHERS SAID THAT SLAVERY ITSELF WAS THE PROBLEM...

MARK TWAIN SAID IT HAPPENED BECAUSE THE SOUTH HAD READ TOO MANY NOVELS BY SIR WALTER SCOTT...

HAVING MADE SLAVERY LOOK
GOOD (AT LEAST TO THEMSELVES),
THE SLAVEOWNERS WENT ON
TO MAKE FREE LABOR
SOUND BAD... FREE WORKERS
WERE TOO FOND OF STRIKES,
THEY SAID, WHEREAS SLAVES WERE
MORE ATTACHED TO
BALLS...

BY CHAINS,
THAT IS...

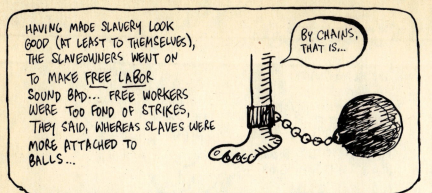

THEY ENVISIONED
A GLORIOUS AMERICAN
FUTURE IN WHICH
ALL WORKERS,
NORTH, SOUTH,
BLACK AND WHITE,
WOULD BE ENSLAVED!!

PLEASE...
JUST GIVE
SLAVERY A
CHANCE TO
COMPETE...

ONE THING YOU CAN
SAY FOR THE PRO-
SLAVERY PROPAGANDISTS:
THEY WEREN'T TRYING
TO BE POPULAR!!

WE MUST
HAVE A WAR
NOW AND DESTROY
THESE PEOPLE...

THEN, JUST TO PROVE
THAT A CLEVER PERSON
CAN DEFEND ANYTHING,
THE SLAVEOWNERS TRIED
TO PROVE THAT
SLAVERY IS A **GOOD**
THING. IN THE
FIRST PLACE, THEY ARGUED,
BLACKS HAD BEEN GIVEN
A FREE TRIP FROM
HEATHEN AFRICA TO
CHRISTIAN AMERICA!

ALL THIS TALK OF
MISERABLE SLAVES
WAS FALSE, THEY SAID...
THE SLAVES WERE
HAPPY — JUST ASK
THEM (IN MASTER'S
PRESENCE, OF COURSE!)...

AND BECAUSE THE WORD "SLAVERY"
SOUNDED SO BAD, THEY LOOKED
FOR ANOTHER NAME FOR IT...
WHAT THEY CAME UP WITH
WAS "THE SOUTH'S PECULIAR
INSTITUTION..."

AS USUAL, WHEN THE
SOUTH FELT WRONGED,
NORTHERNERS AND SOUTHERNERS
SCREAMED AT EACH OTHER
UNTIL THEIR VOICES GAVE OUT
AND THEN ARRANGED THE

COMPROMISE OF 1850,

WHICH —

⭐ ADMITTED CALIFORNIA TO THE UNION AS A FREE STATE...

⭐ OPENED UTAH TO SLAVERY — IF ITS CITIZENS APPROVED...

⭐ BANNED SLAVE MARKETS FROM WASHINGTON, D.C...

⭐ PASSED A TOUGH FUGITIVE SLAVE LAW...

⭐ CHOPPED OFF A PIECE OF TEXAS, AND GAVE IT
TO NEW MEXICO.

TRADE CALIFORNIA FOR UTAH?!! THANKS A HEAP!!

WHENEVER THE COUNTRY EXPANDED, NORTH AND SOUTH HAD MADE COMPROMISES... THE MOST RECENT HAVING BEEN THE MISSOURI COMPROMISE OF 1820. THIS ADMITTED MISSOURI AS A SLAVE STATE, WHILE LIMITING FUTURE SLAVE STATES TO THE AREA SOUTH OF MISSOURI'S SOUTHERN BORDER. NOW, IN 1850, THE COUNTRY HAD REACHED THE PACIFIC... CALIFORNIA WANTED TO BE A FREE STATE... AND SLAVEOWNERS GASPED AT WHAT WAS LEFT FOR THEM:

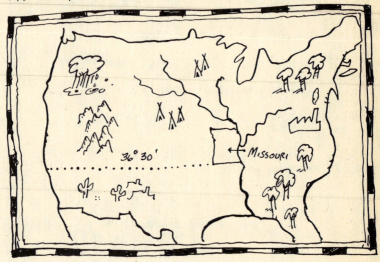

...NAMELY, ARIZONA AND NEW MEXICO!

161

WHEN THIS FAILED TO MELT
CUBAN HEARTS, THE SOUTH
SWITCHED FROM SALIVA TO
SALINA, AS IN **KANSAS**.

IN 1854, CONGRESS OPENED
KANSAS TO "POPULAR SOVEREIGNTY,"
MEANING THAT THE QUESTION OF
SLAVERY IN KANSAS WOULD
BE DECIDED BY THE PEOPLE
OF KANSAS.

ABOLITIONISTS AND PRO-SLAVERY
MILITANTS RUSHED IN, BLASTING
EACH OTHER AS THEY WENT, ON
THE OUTMODED MEDICAL THEORY
THAT BLEEDING ANYTHING, EVEN
KANSAS, WAS THERAPEUTIC...

SINCE UTAH DIDN'T
LOOK MUCH
BETTER THAN
ARIZONA,
SOUTHERNERS
TRIED TO
EXPAND IN OTHER
DIRECTIONS...
AND WHAT
BETTER DIRECTION
THAN SOUTH?
TENNESSEEAN

WILLIAM WALKER

RODE INTO (YES!)
NICAGUA AND
PROCLAIMED HIMSELF
PRESIDENT!

THE NICARAGUANS
WERE BETTER
SHOTS THAN
HOSTS, SO
WALKER'S HORSE
HAD TO LEAVE
WITHOUT HIM...

OTHER SOUTHERNERS
BEGAN DROOLING
OVER CUBA...

163

THIS TURMOIL
PRODUCED, IN THE
NORTH, A NEW
POLITICAL PARTY, THE

REPUBLICANS.

(EVER SINCE JACKSON,
THE ORIGINAL JEFFERSONIAN
REPUBLICANS WERE
CALLED "DEMOCRATS.")
THE REPUBLICANS HAD
A SINGLE PRINCIPLE:

THIS IS ONE MORE PRINCIPLE THAN MOST POLITICAL PARTIES!

IT WAS: NO SLAVERY IN THE TERRITORIES.

WITHIN A FEW YEARS,
THE REPUBLICANS
WERE A MAJOR
PARTY. HOW DO
WE ACCOUNT FOR
THIS INSTANT SUCCESS,
CONSIDERING THAT
AMERICA IS A
GRAVEYARD OF
MINOR PARTIES?

FREE SOIL PARTY

AMERICAN PARTY

BULL MOOSE

PROHIBITION PARTY

WHO'S NEXT? HEE HEE

WHAT WAS ITS
APPEAL? WHERE WAS
THE SELF-INTEREST
OF WHITE VOTERS IN
AN ANTI-SLAVERY
PARTY? WAS IT
JUST BECAUSE IT
MADE THEM FEEL
VIRTUOUS?

VIRTUE
POLITICAL GRAVEYARD
SELF-INTEREST
WASHINGTON, D.C.

MEANWHILE, THERE WAS THAT "FUGITIVE SLAVE" LAW, DESIGNED TO RETURN RUNAWAYS TO THE SOUTH... AND WHAT A LAW IT WAS! IT DENIED THE ACCUSED ANY RIGHT TO A JURY TRIAL, OR EVEN TO TESTIFY IN SELF-DEFENSE... IT EVEN PAID THE JUDGE DOUBLE FOR FINDING IN FAVOR OF THE MASTER! UNDER THE CIRCUMSTANCES, MANY NORTHERN BLACKS, EVEN FREE ONES, DECIDED THAT THERE WAS ONLY ONE THING TO DO — PACK!!

WHILE HUNDREDS, IF NOT THOUSANDS, FLED INTO CANADA, OTHERS RISKED FINES, INJURY, AND JAIL BY STORMING THE PRISONS TO FREE ARRESTED FUGITIVES...

A TYPICAL, IF ESPECIALLY ELOQUENT, REPUBLICAN WAS THE ILLINOIS LAWYER **ABRAHAM LINCOLN.** BORN IN 1809, HE WAS CONVINCED BY THE EVENTS OF THE '50's THAT SLAVERY MUST SPREAD NO FARTHER... BUT HE OPPOSED ITS ABOLITION IN THE SOUTH ON CONSTITUTIONAL GROUNDS... AND HE WAS ENTIRELY UNCERTAIN WHAT TO DO ABOUT FREE BLACKS.

"LET US UNITE AS ONE PEOPLE..."

"I AM NOT... IN FAVOR OF MAKING VOTERS OF THE FREE NEGROES."

IN THE 1858 SENATE RACE, LINCOLN MADE A NAME FOR HIMSELF IN A SERIES OF DEBATES WITH THE INCUMBENT DEMOCRAT **STEPHEN DOUGLAS.** DOUGLAS

TOOK THE "POPULAR SOVEREIGNTY" POSITION THAT HAD ALREADY DRENCHED KANSAS IN BLOOD. LINCOLN TOOK THE REPUBLICAN LINE THAT SLAVERY, AS A WRONG, MUST BE STOPPED — AS FAR AS THE CONSTITUTION ALLOWED.

DESPITE DOUGLAS' EXPERIENCE AND REPUTATION, LINCOLN NEARLY WON THE ELECTION, AND THE SOUTH TOOK NOTE!

HE SURELY HAS MADE A NAME FOR HIMSELF...

CAIN'T SAY WHAT IT IS IN A FAMILY PUBLICATION...

THE REPUBLICANS SUCCEEDED BECAUSE THEY BILLED THEMSELVES AS THE PARTY OF THE

FREE, WHITE, WORKING MAN.

HEY, THAT'S ME!

THE WESTERN TERRITORIES WERE SEEN AS THE LAND OF OPPORTUNITY FOR WHITE WORKERS. THEREFORE, ARGUED THE REPUBLICANS, SLAVERY MUST BE KEPT OUT OF THEM!!

OR WE'LL END UP LIKE POOR WHITES DOWN SOUTH!

SLAVERY, THEY SAID, WAS WRONG NOT ONLY BECAUSE OF WHAT IT DID TO BLACKS, BUT BECAUSE OF WHAT IT DID TO THE WHITE WORKER.

IT'S UNFAIR COMPETITION!

THIS LOGIC CARRIED MANY REPUBLICANS EVEN FURTHER — TO THE POINT OF EXCLUDING EVEN FREE BLACKS FROM THE TERRITORIES. AFTER ALL, "EVERYONE KNEW" THAT BLACKS WOULD WORK FOR LOWER WAGES THAN WHITES!

THE 4 MILLION SLAVES FORMED A LOW-PAID LABOR POOL, WHICH COMPETED WITH FREE WORKERS. THE SLAVE SYSTEM LOWERED WAGES, RAISED HOURS, ERODED WORKING CONDITIONS, AND DESTROYED THE CONCEPT OF THE DIGNITY OF LABOR.

WHY IS THAT?

BECAUSE FREE WHITE EMPLOYERS PAY US LESS!

AND SO, WITH THE COUNTRY IN A STATE (INSTEAD OF THE OTHER WAY AROUND, WHICH IS NORMAL), THERE CAME THE ELECTION OF

1860.

AS THEIR PRESIDENTIAL CANDIDATE, THE REPUBLICANS CHOSE ABRAHAM LINCOLN... HE WASN'T THE MOST PROMINENT MAN IN THE PARTY, BUT HE HAD THE MOST PROMINENT NOSE...

AN OBSCURE MAN WITHOUT ENEMIES...

LINCOLN REALLY WAS BORN IN A LOG CABIN... A TOO-TALL, BACKWOODS LAWYER WHO TOLD CORNY JOKES AT THE WRONG TIME... A CAREER POLITICIAN WHO HAD NEVER RISEN HIGHER THAN THE HOUSE OF REPRESENTATIVES... IN SHORT, AN OBVIOUS LOSER...

DEMOCRATS, REJOICE!!

BUT THE DEMOCRATS HYSTERICALLY SPLIT INTO NORTHERN AND SOUTHERN WINGS AND NOMINATED TWO CANDIDATES —

WITH THE RESULT THAT LINCOLN WON THE ELECTION WITH 40% OF THE POPULAR VOTE!!

IF THE REPUBLICANS PLANNED TO LIMIT SLAVERY TO THE SOUTH, THE SOUTHERNERS NOW DEMANDED TO PUSH IT INTO THE NORTH!

AIN'T NOTHIN' IN THE CONSTITUTION AGIN' IT!

* * * * * * * * * * *
IN 1857, THE SOUTHERN-DOMINATED SUPREME COURT, UNDER ANDREW JACKSON'S OLD PAL, CHIEF JUSTICE ROGER TANEY, MADE THE DRED SCOTT DECISION, WHICH DENIED CONGRESS THE RIGHT TO RESTRICT SLAVERY ANYWHERE.
* * * * * * * * * *

⇒ BLACKS, WROTE TANEY, HAD "NO RIGHTS WHICH THE WHITE MAN IS BOUND TO RESPECT."

THE INFURIATED MILITANT ABOLITIONIST JOHN BROWN LED AN INTERRACIAL RAID ON A VIRGINIA ARSENAL, HOPING TO SPARK A SLAVE INSURRECTION. THE SPARK FIZZLED... NOBODY INSURRECTED... AND BROWN WAS HANGED ON DEC. 2, 1859.

OBSERVED BY BLACKS AS "MARTYR'S DAY"!

AND NOW THAT THE SOUTH HAD RISEN IN REBELLION, LINCOLN COULD FREE THE SLAVES, RIGHT?

THE REPUBLICANS SAID THEY HATED SLAVERY AND ALL THAT... ITS SPREAD SHOULD BE STOPPED... BUT ABOLISH IT WHERE IT ALREADY EXISTED? THAT WOULD BE UNCONSTITUTIONAL!!

NO... THIS WAS A WAR TO SAVE THE UNION, NOT TO ABOLISH SLAVERY!

"IF I COULD SAVE THE UNION WITHOUT FREEING ANY SLAVE, I WOULD DO IT; AND IF I COULD DO IT BY FREEING ALL THE SLAVES, I WOULD DO IT."

TO THIS, THE ABOLITIONISTS BELLOWED THAT SLAVERY WAS THE CAUSE OF THE WAR, AND AS LONG AS THERE WAS SLAVERY, THERE WOULD BE NO PEACE...

"WE HAVE ATTEMPTED TO MAINTAIN OUR UNION IN DEFIANCE OF THE MORAL CHEMISTRY OF THE UNIVERSE," WROTE FREDERICK DOUGLASS.

EVEN BEFORE HE WAS SWORN IN, LINCOLN WAS SWORN AT, MOSTLY BY THE SOUTHERN STATES... WHEN HE DIDN'T SWEAR BACK, THE SOUTH ASSUMED THERE WAS NO FIGHT IN THE MAN... AND THE WHOLE REGION PARTED WAYS WITH THE NORTH.

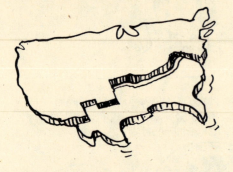

IT CALLED ITSELF THE **CONFEDERATE STATES OF AMERICA**, A NATION DEDICATED TO THE PRINCIPLE THAT ANY STATE HAD A RIGHT TO SECEDE FROM IT...

ITS PRESIDENT WAS **JEFFERSON DAVIS** OF MISSISSIPPI, A MAN AS FIRM AS LINCOLN, BUT WITHOUT ABE'S INCREDIBLE ABILITY TO MAKE PEOPLE LIKE HIM...

AND WHAT DID LINCOLN DO? HE LET HIS BEARD GROW!

LINCOLN, WHO WAS IN FACT A CHAMPIONSHIP WRESTLER, WAS WISELY WAITING FOR THE SOUTH TO MAKE THE FIGHTING MOVE!

ON APRIL 12, 1861, THE GOOD CITIZENS OF CHARLESTON, S.C., BEGAN TO BOMBARD THE U.S. FORT (SUMTER), AND THE WAR WAS ON...

171

LINCOLN INVITED FREDERICK DOUGLASS TO THE WHITE HOUSE. ("I FOUND HIM SEATED WITH HIS FEET IN DIFFERENT PARTS OF THE ROOM," DOUGLASS WROTE.)

THE ABOLITIONIST ACCUSED THE PRESIDENT OF VACILLATION AND SLOWNESS... HE URGED HIM TO ABOLISH SLAVERY AND ENLIST BLACKS IN THE ARMY...

LINCOLN ADMITTED BEING SLOW, BUT DENIED EVER HAVING WAVERED...

DOUGLASS WAS IMPRESSED... SO WAS LINCOLN...

BY THE END OF 1862, LINCOLN HAD ISSUED THE ⇒ EMANCIPATION PROCLAMATION,

WHICH FREED THE SLAVES — IF ONLY IN REBEL-HELD TERRITORIES...

FREE AT LAST!

YEH... IF THE UNION ARMY EVER ARRIVES...

174

THE WORSE IT WENT FOR THE NORTH, THE BETTER THE ABOLITIONISTS SOUNDED— AND IT WAS GOING BADLY, AS THE SOUTH WON BATTLE AFTER BATTLE..

THE SOUTH, THOUGH OUTNUMBERED, HAD GREAT GENERALS: ROBERT E. LEE AND STONEWALL JACKSON.

THE NORTH HAD GEORGE McCLELLAN, WHOSE MEN LOVED HIM, BECAUSE HE RARELY RISKED THEIR LIVES.

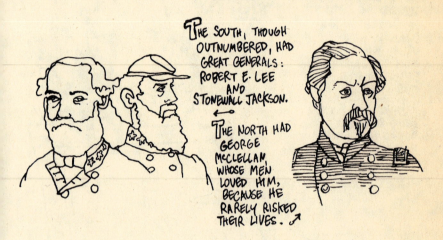

AS THE GRAYS CONTINUED TO WHIP THE BLUES, THE UNION WAS FORCED TO TURN TO THE BLACKS...

173

JUST THEN,
ALMOST MIRACULOUSLY,
THE TIDE BEGAN TO
TURN, BUT SLOWLY...
ONE REASON WAS
THE BLACK TROOPS
PUSHING UP FROM THE
DEEP SOUTH...
ANOTHER WAS THE
DEATH OF STONEWALL
JACKSON, SHOT
ACCIDENTALLY BY HIS
OWN MEN, WHO THEN
DROPPED THE STRETCHER...

ANOTHER WAS A NAVAL BLOCKADE OF SOUTHERN PORTS... ANOTHER WAS THE CAPTURE OF NEW ORLEANS... ANOTHER WAS THE FEROCIOUS UNION DRIVE DOWN THE MISSISSIPPI, WHICH SPLIT THE SOUTH AND ALLOWED THE BLUES TO PENETRATE THE CONFEDERACY FROM THE WEST...

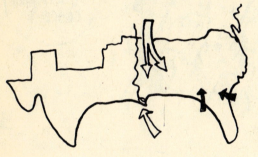

(NOTE: ALMOST
ALL THE FIGHTING
TOOK PLACE IN
THE SOUTH...)

OUT OF THE WEST
STAGGERED
GENERAL
ULYSSES S.
GRANT.

A HARD DRINKER... A
FAILURE AS A CIVILIAN...
AN ANTI-SEMITE... BUT
HE WON BATTLES...

176

AT THE SAME TIME, BLACKS— FREE NORTHERNERS AND ESCAPED SLAVES — WERE FINALLY ALLOWED INTO THE ARMY... IN ALL-BLACK REGIMENTS, OF COURSE!

TO THE SURPRISE OF SOME, THEY TURNED OUT TO BE AMONG THE NORTH'S BEST TROOPS, AND NO WONDER — THEY WERE THE MOST MOTIVATED!

WHEN THEY MARCHED THROUGH THE SOUTH, SLAVES DESERTED THE PLANTATIONS IN DROVES, LEAVING THEIR DRIVERS HOLDING THE STEERING WHEEL...

175

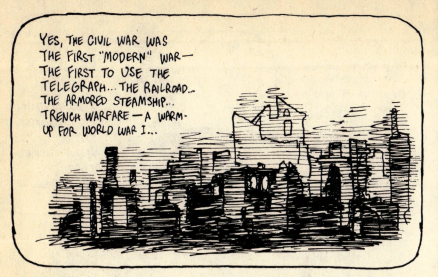

YES, THE CIVIL WAR WAS THE FIRST "MODERN" WAR — THE FIRST TO USE THE TELEGRAPH... THE RAILROAD... THE ARMORED STEAMSHIP... TRENCH WARFARE — A WARM-UP FOR WORLD WAR I...

...WHERAS NUCLEAR WAR IS MORE POST-MODERN...

THE CIVIL WAR ALSO BROUGHT THE FIRST INCOME TAX... THE FIRST "GREENBACKS" (I.E., PAPER MONEY BACKED ONLY BY THE COLOR OF INK IT WAS PRINTED WITH)...

AND THE FIRST TIME THE GOVERNMENT EVER BORROWED $3 BILLION — A REGULAR "DANCE OF DEBT."

BUT NOT THE LAST!

IN 1864, LINCOLN PUT GRANT IN CHARGE OF ALL THE UNION ARMIES...

GO... FINISH 'EM OFF... IT'S 3 YEARS ALREADY...

GRANT WAS NO MATCH FOR LEE WHEN IT CAME TO MANEUVERABILITY AND IMAGINATION, BUT HE HAD A WINNING TACTIC ALL HIS OWN—

NAMELY, A WAR OF ATTRITION, IN WHICH BODIES PILED UP UNTIL ONE SIDE RAN OUT...

(IN THE TRENCH WARFARE BEFORE RICHMOND, SOLDIERS WENT INTO BATTLE WITH THEIR NAMES AND ADDRESSES PINNED TO THEIR BACKS, FOR E-Z CLEAN-UP...)

AFTER 80,000 PERISHED IN ONE ESPECIALLY LONG BATTLE, GENERAL LEE REALIZED THAT HE WAS FACING A 20TH-CENTURY GENERAL IN THE 19TH CENTURY, WHILE DEFENDING AN 18TH-CENTURY INSTITUTION. LACKING A TIME MACHINE, LEE SURRENDERED, AND THE WAR WAS OVER.

NOW CAN WE HAVE THE COMPROMISE OF 1865?

177

BIBLIOGRAPHY

Bailey, T.A., *THE AMERICAN PAGEANT*, 4th Edition, Lexington, HEATH, 1971; A FAT, STANDARD, SELF-SATISFIED TEXT

Bayliss, J.F. *BLACK SLAVE NARRATIVES*, N.Y., MACMILLAN, 1970

Brailsford, H.N., *THE LEVELLERS & THE ENGLISH REVOLUTION*, PALO ALTO, STANFORD, 1961

Billings, Warren, *THE OLD DOMINION IN THE SEVENTEENTH CENTURY*, CHAPEL HILL, U. OF N. CAROLINA PRESS, 1975; GOOD INSIGHTS INTO OLD VIRGINNY

Brodie, F., *NO MAN KNOWS MY HISTORY*, 2nd Edition, N.Y., KNOPF, 1972; THE AMAZING STORY OF JOSEPH SMITH, FOUNDER OF MORMONISM

Brodie, F., *THOMAS JEFFERSON, AN INTIMATE HISTORY*, N.Y., NORTON, 1974; THE LIFE & LOVES OF OUR FUN-LOVING FOUNDING FATHER

Caulfield, C., *THE IRON WILL OF JEFFERSON DAVIS*, N.Y., HARCOURT, BRACE, JOVANOVICH, 1978

Coleman, R.J., *LIBERTY AND PROPERTY*, N.Y., SCRIBNER'S, 1951; A GOOD, OLD-FASHIONED NARRATIVE OF COLONIAL TIMES

Davis, W.C., *THE DEEP WATERS OF THE PROUD* (3 VOLS) N.Y., DOUBLEDAY, 1982-'83; THE COMPLETE CIVIL WAR

Douglass, F., *NARRATIVE OF THE LIFE OF FREDERICK DOUGLASS, AN AMERICAN SLAVE*, CAMBRIDGE, MA, HARVARD, 1960; THE SECTION ON PLANTATION MUSIC IS ESPECIALLY POWERFUL

Edmunds, R.D., *TECUMSEH AND THE QUEST FOR INDIAN LEADERSHIP*, BOSTON, LITTLE BROWN, 1984

Foner, P., ED., *LIFE AND WRITINGS OF FREDERICK DOUGLASS*, N.Y., INTERNATIONAL PUBLISHERS, 1950; DO YOURSELF A FAVOR & SAMPLE THIS BRILLIANT PROSE!

Greene, L.J., *THE NEGRO IN COLONIAL NEW ENGLAND 1620-1776*, PORT WASHINGTON, KENNIKAT PRESS, 1966; A NEGLECTED SUBJECT

Higginson, T.W., *ARMY LIFE IN A BLACK REGIMENT*, MICHIGAN STATE U., 1960; CIVIL WAR CLASSIC

Hughes, L., Meltzer, M., AND Lincoln, C.E., *A PICTORIAL HISTORY OF BLACK AMERICANS*, N.Y., CROWN, 1973

Hulton, P., ED., *AMERICA 1585*, CHAPEL HILL, U. OF N. CAROLINA PRESS, 1984; THE STUNNING WATERCOLORS BY JOHN WHITE, GOVERNOR OF THE "LOST COLONY"

James, M., *THE LIFE OF ANDREW JACKSON*, N.Y., BOBBS-MERRILL, 1938; MUST BE READ TO BE BELIEVED!

Ketcham, R., *BENJAMIN FRANKLIN*, N.Y., WASHINGTON SQ. PRESS, 1966

Longford, Earl of, *ABRAHAM LINCOLN*, N.Y., PUTNAM, 1975

Lynd, S., *CLASS CONFLICT, SLAVERY, & THE UNITED STATES CONSTITUTION*, N.Y., BOBBS-MERRILL, 1967; A PENETRATING ANALYSIS

Rowbotham, S., *HIDDEN FROM HISTORY*, N.Y., PANTHEON, 1974; THE IMPACT OF THE INDUSTRIAL REVOLUTION ON FAMILY LIFE

Schroeder, J.H., *MR. POLK'S WAR*, MADISON, U. OF WISCONSIN PRESS, 1973; THE POLITICS BEHIND AMERICA'S LEAST-KNOWN WAR

Trollope, F., *DOMESTIC MANNERS OF THE AMERICANS*, N.Y., OXFORD U. PRESS, 1984; EYEWITNESS ACCOUNT FROM 1832

Wilson, R.R., *LINCOLN IN CARICATURE*, N.Y., HORIZON, 1953; A REMINDER THAT LINCOLN WAS LAMPOONED

Wright, T., *A CARICATURE HISTORY OF THE GEORGES*, LONDON, CHATTO & WINDAM, 1904; 18th C. ENGLAND THRU THE EYES OF CARTOONISTS—A FORGOTTEN MASTERPIECE

Zinn, H., *A PEOPLE'S HISTORY OF THE UNITED STATES*, N.Y., HARPER & ROW, 1980; POLEMICAL & ICONOCLASTIC

AND ABRAHAM LINCOLN — WHO HAD RISEN FROM POVERTY TO THE PRESIDENCY... WHO BEGAN AS THE CHAMPION OF THE FREE, WHITE WORKER AND BECAME THE LIBERATOR OF THE SLAVES... WHO ADMIRED JEFFERSON ABOVE ALL AND DESTROYED JEFFERSON'S OLD SOUTH... WHO ENDURED BEING ATTACKED AS A BUFFOON, A BABOON, AN INCOMPETENT, AND A TYRANT... WHOSE WONDERFUL SENSE OF HUMOR MASKED A PROFOUND SADNESS... WHO BELIEVED THAT HE HAD BEEN CONTROLLED BY EVENTS... LINCOLN, TOO, BECAME A "FIRST."

THE FIRST PRESIDENT TO BE ASSASSINATED.

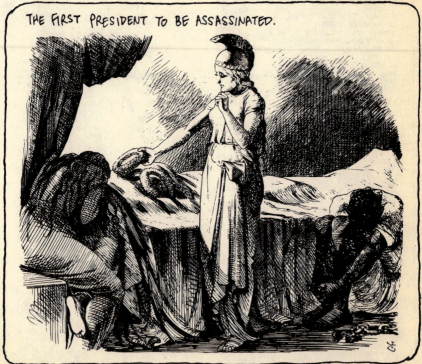

TO BE CONTINUED...

INDEX

ABOUT THE AUTHOR

LARRY GONICK, THE OVEREDUCATED CARTOONIST, HAS BEEN WRITING AND DRAWING CARTOON HISTORIES SINCE THE EARLY 1970'S. HE LIVES IN SAN FRANCISCO WITH HIS WIFE, DAUGHTER, AND COLLECTION OF HISTORICAL RELICS.

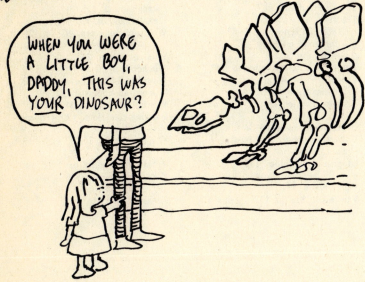

185